Luther Now

HANNS LILJE

Luther

Now

Translated by
CARL J. SCHINDLER

MUHLENBERG PRESS, Philadelphia

Translated from Luther
By Hanns Lilje
Lätare Verlag, Nürnberg, 1946

Printed in U. S. A.

UB720

Translator's Preface

During the past two decades countless people in many lands have suffered at the hands of dictators because as individualists and humanitarians they were staunchly opposed to the policies of totalitarian regimes.

Dr. Hanns Lilje shared their fate, not as a nineteenth century liberal but as a Christian whose opposition to tyranny grew out of his devotion to the gospel and Luther's theology. The importance of this book lies in the fact that the author knows Luther's thought world as intimately as he knows the modern mind. He is profoundly conscious of the conflict between these two fundamentally different philosophies of life, and the many attempts to resolve it by the assertion that Protestantism and liberalism have essentially the same aims and arrive at the same conclusions. Dr. Lilje rejects this synthesis. He carefully disentangles the strains of Reformation thinking and modern individualism, and offers his own interpretation of the contribution that Luther can make to the religiously barren civilization of the twentieth century.

This is in every respect a European book. No one but a European, who is deeply steeped in the intellectual traditions of the Old World and shaken to the core by the apparent "Decline of the West," could have written it. Much in this book will startle the American reader, and with some of its conclusions he will be inclined to disagree. The author's attitude toward the state will surprise those who have learned their political philosophy from Locke, Jefferson, and Rousseau.

The very fact that this book comes from the other side of the Atlantic, and remains a German book even in translation, makes its appearance timely. It introduces us to certain aspects of the Reformation which we ordinarily overlook because our political, social, and intellectual heritage has been different. We know little of the "anguish of existence" or the feeling that the "age of the church" is over, because we have never known a state church. Bishop Lilje enables us to see the contemporary scene through the eyes of a brilliant, consecrated scholar and churchman. It is an informative book; perchance it might even be a prophetic book.

Carl J. Schindler

Contents

PART III

Introduction

Luther presents the unique case of a man whose intensely personal religious experience has affected the course of history more profoundly than the life work of any king, general, statesman, or business magnate.

With a few regrettable exceptions all men now enjoy night after night the glow of the incandescent lamp, which Edison's inventive genius has given to mankind. Yet, is there anyone who would seriously compare Edison's contribution with that of Luther? In those concerns which are most characteristically human, beginning with faith and ending with the social order, the state, the family, the legal institutions, no influence within the last four hundred years has equaled that of Luther.

It is therefore the more amazing that no one seems to know him very well. This neglect is world-wide. With the exception of John Wesley and Thomas Carlyle, the Anglo-Saxon world has never paid much attention to him. It has traditionally looked upon him as a German theologian. It is as much taken for granted that every German is a Lutheran as one assumes that every Englishman is without doubt an Anglican. The man who stands at the very beginning of these great changes in Christendom is rarely considered. English literature about Luther and German Protestantism is indeed scanty.

The fact is well recognized that the Latins do not know him. Even Pascal, a thinker whose speculations often approached closely to the thinking of the Reformers, found Luther too overpowering and illogical for his precise, fastidious French mind. He protests: *Tout hors le vrai* (Everything except the truth). More serious is the fact that even his own countrymen no longer know him. Germans were overtaken by a tidal wave of intellectualism before they had learned to understand the man for whom the church is named to which so many of them belong.

This book is not intended as a vindication of Luther's place in history; that problem has been discussed in many books. The sixteenth century—this zenith in German history—has been so minutely examined by historians, by friend and foe, that no stone has remained unturned. The picture of the epoch as we have it now is not likely to be materially affected by any future scientific investigation. In this study we are not concerned with historical research but with applied history, so to speak, not with judgments about the past but the present. We only offer a historical summary, because like a traveler we want to glance backward from time to time to make sure that we are proceeding in the right direction. There is ample justification for such a procedure. The spiritual history of Europe has now approached a vast abyss which opens menacingly before it. A new form of nihilism is arising. The fact that many people underestimate the seriousness of the situation does not relieve it but aggravates it.

In his autobiography, published in 1922, Mussolini made a pertinent statement which later events have borne out: "At the present time there exist three world powers. The British Empire comprises large territorial possessions but no longer has a common philosophy to bind them together. The Russian Empire seeks expansion in the East for the elaboration of its ideology. The third is the 'invisible Kingdom of Christ.' Of these three 'the little ship of the divine Hebrew' still sails most securely upon the waves of time and will probably do so in the future." Everyone will admit that "the ideology from the East" is a reality. It is equally evident that it is aggressive and advances steadily by propaganda and military strategy. The inevitable question, how far the West is prepared to meet this challenge cannot be answered unequivocally. The West appears to be far more helpless than we had realized. That is one of the many reasons why inquiries into the spiritual nature of the West are so necessary. British statesmen in their public utterances have asked the students at Oxford and Cambridge for years to examine the cultural foundations of English life, and that really means to think about the Christian faith. In the meantime the situation has become increasingly critical. Our striving for some clarification regarding the spiritual foundations of Europe is no longer merely a literary concern. One should not look upon such an undertaking simply as an attempt to reassure the Christian world about its future. Whatever the external fate of the church will be in the future, the true church knows that together with the gospel she has also received the divine promise that even the gates of hell shall not prevail against her. She knows it, as far as she has any real understanding of the faith whose guardian she has been for nearly two thousand years. But this promise obviously makes no reference to her external existence. It does not claim that her future will be spectacular or that she will win all men. Neither does the divine promise indicate any kind of certainty for the political destinies of Europe or Germany. The nations of Europe may not even have enough strength left to return to the foundations which have given Europe its historical distinctiveness in the past. Because it is as impossible to disregard the laws of the spirit as the laws of nature, the West has for some time experienced the fateful consequences of its spiritual indifference. Under the impact of the remarkable, often over-whelming achievements of science and industry, the claims of faith were first relegated to a secondary place and finally ignored altogether. Metaphysical thinking declined. The ability to believe, truly to believe, has almost ceased in the West, and more is needed in this crucial hour than a revival of the traditional idealistic philosophies of the past.

This question about the future is so urgent that little needs to be said about it. Without some certainty regarding the spiritual future, there can be no political future. In every case, so far, spiritual nihilism has been the forerunner of political nihilism and total collapse.

If Europe is not really exhausted it must retain its European characteristics and derive its strength from the forces that originally brought it into being. It is no longer the question which Burckhardt[1] asked so anxiously on behalf of the civilized European and answered so pessimistically: "How long will our Western ideals be able to remain afloat?", but it has now become the far more serious question: "Is Europe able to live at all?" It is neither sentimentalism nor theological apologetic but the adduction of an undeniable historical fact that Europe cannot remain what it was if the drift away from Christianity continues; at the moment it appears as though that trend were well established. Only a dilettante can claim that a new faith strong enough to replace the old has already made its appearance. Are there still contemporaries who seriously expect a new dawn under the banner of Rosenberg and Ludendorff?[2] As long as our

---

[1] Jacob Burckhardt (1818-97) Swiss historian, professor at the University of Basle. He wrote regarding the history of art and civilization.

[2] Chief exponents of a "Germanic Religion" in the Third Reich of Adolf Hitler. They called for the abolition of "the myth of the twentieth century," i.e. Christianity, and the adoption of a new faith based upon German mythology and folklore. (Tr.)

fate is still in the making, any attempt to regain our basic premises appears worth while.

That is the reason we inquire into the work of Martin Luther and its significance for the West. We do not ask our questions for the sake of pure scholarship or the discovery of some historical details, but as people who are aware of the deadly malady that is spreading throughout the Western world.

To be an objective historian, while one is at the same time searching for an answer to our present dilemma, is a difficult twofold task, and one may even question whether such an approach is possible or still worth while.

We must start with the realization that Luther is in many respects a product of the late Middle Ages. His mental processes, his opinions about the nature of the universe, his historical judgments, his knowledge of geography, economics, social problems were those which prevailed everywhere during that period. It was, of course, no longer the world of the high Middle Ages. Luther had already learned during his student days that the world is round, and from progressive scientists of his day he had acquired a distaste for alchemy and that "shoddy art"—astrology. It serves no purpose to minimize Luther's medieval heritage by forcing him to think in terms of the twentieth century and searching through his extensive writings for proof of his modernity.

How difficult it is to judge out of one's own contemporary situation and still do justice to the sixteenth century, is well illustrated by some nineteenth century scholars. Though the nineteenth century is the classical age of historical scholarship, four of its outstanding representatives expressed amazingly prejudiced views about the Reformation. We are speaking of Kierkegaard, Burckhardt, Lagarde, and Nietzsche. Their comments betray a certain nervous irritation; they do not impress the reader as objective conclusions warranted by facts. While their findings differ materially from one another, they are all the outcome of a definite psychological attitude. This irritability is evidence of the great strain that was felt by intellectuals of the late nineteenth century. They keenly felt and candidly admitted that life was rapidly changed by the natural sciences and technical inventions; the age of the machine fixed man's attention upon externals and thereby threatened all spiritual and ideal values. Amidst a self-satisfied bourgeoisie they stood alone and became prophets crying in the wilderness. One can understand their impatience with a church that had in large measure accommodated itself to this middle-class mentality. But that does not alter the fact that they were wrong in their judgment on the Reformation. It poses the question why these great minds, each so discerning in his reasoning, could still arrive at such a totally distorted view of the past. The answer is probably that they were prophets in their own situation. They pronounced judgment on their own age rather than the sixteenth century. That limitation the four men have in common. They can tell us what was wrong with the nineteenth century, but they cannot give us an adequate picture of the Reformation. Their tortuous style still betrays the uneasiness of their minds, and we can detect it if we free ourselves from the amazing fascination which these writers exercise upon our generation.

Though these four great interpreters and misrepresentatives of the Reformation should serve as a warning, our own situation demands this difficult twofold task: we must see in clear historical perspective, yet remain constantly conscious of our present needs and ask the questions which grow out of them. More is needed than a resumption of anti-Catholic polemic. It would be equally unhistorical if the "other side" were precipitously to renew its condemnation of the Reformation.

The two great churches together must do battle for the continued validity of the Christian heritage. The Christian foundations of Europe are threatened. Their common commitment to the Christian faith and ethos unites the two churches as much as the decisions of the sixteenth century have kept them apart. Our task is not the mere repetition of statements that were tossed back and forth four centuries ago but a re-examination of these principles in the light of an entirely new situation.

Part I

The Background

How are we to think of the sixteenth century? Ardent Protestants describe it as a period of disintegration, a time when traditional Catholicism could no longer satisfy the religious needs of man and people longed for a new, vitalized faith in which their homeless souls could find a haven. Equally ardent Catholics reply that the spiritual life of the age had grown into a precious flower, on which the "schism" fell like a killing spring frost. Before we discuss these conflicting views, it may be well to review briefly the course of events.

It is not easy to make a start. One is startled by the procession of great and very great names: Columbus, Erasmus, Duerer, Muenzer, Paracelsus, Michelangelo, Breughel, Machiavelli, Ignatius Loyola, Cortez, Melanchthon, Rabelais, Calvin. As one senses the power which each name represents, one learns to appreciate the outburst of enthusiasm with which Hutten greeted the first decade of the new century: *O Saeculum, o litteras! Juvat vivere!* (It is joy to be alive!) Joy, but also a very intricate business. Morning casts its bright rays over the world of literature and fine arts, but history like the rushing lava of a volcanic eruption moves on the scene in a tangle of complications. Emperors and war lords, popes and kings, fighters for freedom and conspirators, are at work and busier than ever. A new world emerges in the West, literally out of the sea, and attracts not

3

only men of great courage but greedy, cruel adventurers. Their attempt to make Spain the leading power in Europe, by directing a steady flow of gold into its coffers, opens the way for Spain's decline (and incidentally almost wrecks the economy of Europe). The forces of Islam once more break in from the East, and Europe trembles under the terrific blows which they strike against the eastern gates of the empire. The knights renew their activities and some of them rise to great fame as military leaders before feudalism vanishes forever. New life pulsates through the towns. Restlessness is everywhere. Nothing seems stable because the new displaces the old in science, economics, art, literature, politics, and religious beliefs. "This amazing generation," as Burckhardt has described it, enters the century with a mighty upsurge of power and creativeness. Among these new forces is Martin Luther. In order to understand the changes that were taking place at the time he appeared, we must look carefully at this fascinating, ebullient, colorful scene.

The Empire and Europe

Rightfully we begin with the mighty of this earth. History engaged in a rather fantastic plot when it placed three superior rulers simultaneously as chief actors upon the stage of Europe.

Charles V of Habsburg was a grave, dignified man who had himself under complete control, almost all the time. Francis I, the almost constantly uncontrolled, scintillating king of France, might have become a great ruler had he not been so brilliant and desultory. Henry VIII, the most vigorous of them all, was the king with preposterous ideas about royal rights, politics, marriage, and the church.

They were contemporaries: Henry was born in 1491 and Francis in 1494. Both died in 1547, one year after Luther's death. Charles, who opened his very blue eyes in a cradle at Ghent in the portentous year 1500, left the stage of history in 1556 to await death in the monastery at San Yuste. Even more remarkable is the fact that they began their respective reigns in quick succession of one another. Henry was the first; in 1509 he ascended the somewhat shaky throne which his father, with more luck and tenacity than legal rights, had claimed for the Tudors. Francis, a sprightly prince of twenty-one, began his rule in 1515, and Charles became the successor to his father Maximilian in 1518. In 1519 he was chosen German emperor by the prince electors of Germany.

Even the great menacing outsider, Sultan Suliman II

(1520-66), fits so extraordinarily into the picture that the great European political movements during those decades are determined by the same few individuals, together with a number of quickly changing popes.

Another unusual, fortunate incidence is the fact that the three great rulers enjoyed the services of outstanding painters. Charles had at his command the great art of Titian; Francis used the cultivated, sensitive Clouet whose work seems to anticipate the later development of the French school; and Henry employed the great portrait painter Holbein for an annual stipend of sixty pounds. Each of these artists deserves well of posterity, for their paintings enable us to form a very clear picture of the appearance and personalities of these rulers.

They all had a certain shyness in common, which was particularly pronounced during the early years of their reign. Francis I, whom Clouet has portrayed in the glittering white and green uniform of a Renaissance knight seated on a beautiful horse, was undoubtedly a daring soldier and strategist, whose exploits in the beginning gained him European acclaim and considerable success in his long struggle against Charles. In administrative matters, however, he was so unsure of himself that he accepted gratefully the calm, judicious guidance of his mistress, Diane de Poitiers, who was six years older than he.

This motherly woman, also painted by Clouet, gave him the understanding and counsel he needed in his office. If Diane's position at the court proved beneficial to her many relatives and friends, such an arrangement was not offensive by the standards of the age.

Henry of England was extremely uncertain of himself. Outwardly boisterous and domineering, he was controlled by those resolute individuals whom he had raised from often inferior positions and who could manipulate him at will, as long as they respected certain largely psychologically determined conditions. As soon as they made a mistake in their judgment, they were removed as surely as they had caused others to be removed before them. But somebody always managed Henry; as long as he lived he was a tool in somebody's hands.

Charles, too, was timid. That trait was peculiar with the Habsburgs and increased with each generation until it became pathological in the Spanish branch of the family. Charles, however, knew better than his son and successor, Philip II, how to conceal this weakness. He covered it with the impressive cloak of his imperial dignity. His natural reserve found most congenial the court ceremonial of Burgundy, which later developed into the intricate etiquette of the Spanish royal house. These forms were living expressions of his personality. Such solemn dignity enabled him to postpone decisions. In such an atmosphere nothing was ever done in haste. But once he had reached a decision, often after prolonged inward struggle, he insisted with inflexible determination upon its execution. He thus managed to give the impression of a ruler of truly imperial proportions. We shall find later that this dignity was not an altogether empty shell.

For a moment we compare the facial features of the three rulers. Holbein has painted the square face of Henry VIII, framed by a beard and covered with a barret. The dark twinkling eyes betray less tyrannical self-assurance than youthful shrewdness. We have stated already that this boisterous, blustering man—"mischief-maker and devil at the same time," Burckhardt has called him—was basically a very insecure person. For that very reason one cannot discern any consistent policy during his reign, and it is one of those paradoxes of history that he, of all people, should have started England on the road by which it finally became a great power. It is characteristic of his life that his achievements were always vastly different from his intentions. What a life his was! The king, no longer a young man, is surrounded by his companions as he rests before the flickering fire after a long hard day at the hunt, a sport he enjoyed to the last. The ailing leg pains him and must be propped up. As the cups are passed around, it would have been an opportune time to relax and reflect, but this man has no capacity or will ever to think seriously. He still boastfully claimed the title "King of England and France" long after the French possessions were lost. The pope had honored him as a *defensor fidei,* though he had attacked the faith more often than he had defended it. There had been many marriages and many executions. There had been countless theological disputes with varying and often contradictory decisions: for Protestantism and for the papacy, for separation from Rome and for the celebration of the mass. The man of many marriages insisted obstinately upon the celibacy of the clergy. In his political moves he sided with France one day, with the emperor the next day, but these moves always benefited England. Luther was quite right when he called him a "buffoon" (*Hanswurst*).

In his youth Henry was an affectionate, physically powerful prince, though painfully cowardly in combat. He was sincerely devoted to Catherine of Aragon his first wife who was six years his senior.

It is unfortunate that he combined in his personality a permanent inability to make decisions with a naive, undisguised, crude egoism.

English history in those days was made by backstage politicians, unworthy representatives of their nation, brutal, servile, and unprincipled in their character, but always clever to use every opportunity for personal preferment. The people who rose to prominence at the court are not attractive. One meets Wolsey and Thomas Cromwell, who was so different from his illustrious nephew Oliver. Cranmer was the craven, unprincipled Archbishop of Canterbury. When the king insisted on the celibacy of the clergy, Cranmer dismissed his wife, the niece of the German Reformer Osiander, and secretly sent her back to her native land. Let it be said that courage and dignity came to him at last when he was led to the scaffold. Yet, even the literary beauty of the first part of the *Book of Common Prayer* is no compensation for the lack of integrity in the bearer of such high office. It is the fate of rulers that in their presence common human weaknesses and failings appear in sharper outline. Though these were decisive years in English history they were barren of great personalities.

We can be more brief in our treatment of Francis I. The playboy became king and his career opened under a lucky star. His first daring campaigns yielded him easy victories, but they did not settle the problem that vexed him all his life and shaped French policy for a full century: a settlement with the Habsburgs who pressed France on its southern and northern frontiers.

This daring king fared far worse in war than cautious Henry of England. During the battle of Pavia in 1522 he was captured and spent several humiliating weeks as a prisoner of Charles. Notwithstanding his solemn promises, he immediately resumed hostilities as soon as he was released. Towards the end of his life he became a mature, benign man of the world, who could smile at the escapades of Henry whom he always considered puerile. He started France on the road to becoming a great power, and his successors, notably Henry IV, continued his efforts with remarkable results.

The struggle between Francis and the emperor was long and bitter. Henry always attempted with more or less—usually less—success to reap the benefits that accrue to neutral bystanders. It seems to us that these wars always started over nothing, that they ended as abruptly as they were begun, and that these sacrifices in human blood had no other cause but unbridled dynastic ambitions and jealousies.

In the case of Emperor Charles V it is something more. Even if the participants themselves could not recognize it clearly, they were involved in great decisions that affected the fate of Europe. The empire itself was at stake. Let us examine the personality of the emperor, both as a man and as a ruler. Titian has made two portraits of Charles in very characteristic poses. One shows him on his horse, in full armor, as he surveys the battlefield at Muehlberg. The other is that of a Spanish grandee, seated elegantly in an arm chair. Muehlberg represents the greatest military and political triumph in Charles's career. The battle was fought in 1547, the same year in which his two great rivals had died. The outcome of the battle broke the power of the Protestant princes. It was the last, the most ardently desired triumph in a long line of imperial victories. It seemed to be the climax of his life. Titian showed excellent judgment when he used this moment to immortalize the imperial greatness. But the result of Charles's victories was always problematical. If one inquires which of them had any lasting importance or what was really accomplished, it is almost impossible to give a definite answer.

The other portrait which shows the emperor at Prato is much more realistic. He is seated in an armchair, dressed in the black velvet cloak of a Spanish nobleman; around his neck he wears the chain of the Order of the Golden Fleece and his hand rests upon a small delicate sword. The picture

10

conveys an indelible impression of his personality. Even the unattractive, characteristic Habsburg chin cannot hide the expression of true greatness in this face. However one looks at it, he was by far the greatest among his royal contemporaries, far surpassing them in character, vision, and importance. His moral standards were much higher than those of the other two. Except for slight shadows here and there, he was not tainted by the amorous adventures of the thoughtless Francis and the unrestrained Henry. More important, because it affects his public rather than his private life, is the fact that he had the character of a gentleman. He was conscious of the obligations which a royal promise entails. There is a world of difference between the English king who gave and broke his word at will and the young emperor at Worms, who categorically rejected all suggestions conveniently to dispose of Luther. He had given his imperial pledge and he reminded his entourage that he did not wish to blush as his predecessor Sigismund had to do at Constance.

He emerges, particularly in comparison with the others, as a man of political vision and a real sense of responsibility. Francis I was always a cavalier, a front line officer whose luck held out for a while and failed in the end. Henry operated his realm as a huge private business enterprise and discovered that it paid handsome dividends as long as he was not too meticulous in his dealings. In Charles we find a deep sense of vocation, an awareness of his accountability before God and history.

He was compelled to think in large terms. It was not only a proud boast but an actual fact that the sun never went down in his empire. Spain and Portugal were the two nations for which the discovery of the New World was of immense political importance. Even apart from the demands of an empire that reached beyond the Atlantic, Charles faced extremely complicated tasks in Europe. Henry's kingdom numbered about four million inhabitants. It was an agricultural, self-sufficient society with very limited vision and still deeply steeped in medievalism. Except for a small intellectual aristocracy at Oxford and Cambridge, who cultivated humanistic studies and felt themselves Europeans, the rest of England was nothing more than the northwestern edge of the continent, shrouded in fog, both mentally and physically. France with a population of fourteen million people was far more intimately integrated into the intellectual, cultural, and political history of Europe. Even though the king of France interfered constantly in the political destinies of Europe, particularly Italy, his sphere of influence was puny when we compare it with Charles's gigantic world-wide tasks.

The long struggle with Francis compelled the emperor to give battle in Flanders, Brabant, Burgundy, and more often in Italy. Previously he had to fight in Spain to assure internal order in this far-flung empire. He had gone to war against the Mohammedan pirate states in North Africa, and some of his most decisive victories were won in Algiers.

He was keenly alive to the steadily growing Turkish threat in the East. Who in England would have paid the slightest attention to these Bolsheviks of the sixteenth century who hammered at the eastern gates of the empire? To defend the West against the mounting danger from the East was one of the most important political and military tasks, far more important than the wars of succession or the occasional raids of petty war lords.

The new situation that had been created by the Reformation likewise demanded a solution. Charles felt it his duty to settle this dispute because the movement endangered his political power and the unity of the church, of which he considered himself the secular head. Moderns will find it diffi cult to understand Charles's position. We must realize that he had revived an old concept: the emperor holds the highest temporal office in the church and has therefore certain obligations which he must fulfill to protect the best interests of the Christian world.

Because history is taught in our schools from an exclusively secular point of view, modern students have difficulty in grasping what the term "emperor" really conveyed to the medieval mind. We think immediately of Canossa, of the deliberate humiliation of the empire by the papacy, of the long and bitter contests between the supreme rulers of state and church. But these impressions, which were carefully nurtured by anticlerical nationalists during the nineteenth century, are only partially true and therefore misleading. The unification of the West was the highest spiritual achievement of the Middle Ages. There can be no doubt that the coordination of pope and emperor was always a potential source of conflict and rivalry, but the arrangement had decidedly wholesome effects. It stimulated "an ever more liberating, more comprehensive, deepening movement of the spirit" (Ranke).[1] This great historian of the medieval world reminds us of the striking difference between the West and the Byzantine Empire, where the merging of spiritual and ecclesiastical powers finally produced a hierarchical order as sterile as the similarly constituted caliphate in later Islam.

In the opening years of the sixteenth century the empire was little more than a tradition. Its glory, its importance, the fascination which it once held for the minds of men had

---

[1] Leopold von Ranke (1795-1886), professor of history at the University of Berlin, established history as an "objective science." It is based upon the study of extant documents and the historian derives his material from archives. His task is to "describe what actually happened." Political events constitute for Ranke the core of history. Among his best known works are *The Roman Pontiffs* and *History of Germany in the Age of the Reformation*. (Tr.)

grown dim. When Charles let eleven years go by before he finally consented to accept the imperial crown at the hands of the weakling Pope Clement VII, the long delay bordered on deliberate neglect. It was the last coronation of a German emperor by a pope and for the German people the symbolism had lost almost all significance. Charles's empire had gained immensely in territorial possessions. The German-Spanish realm was now a world empire. But even Charles, the youthful, brilliant emperor, was unable to alter the fact that the empire, though larger in area than ever before, was no longer a spiritual power. Few German princes even bothered to attend the ceremony. It was not sentimentalism which prompted Charles to keep the idea of the empire alive, for this was not a romantic age. But Charles had a profound sense for history and believed all his life that the responsibility for the unity of the faith rested upon the emperor as the secular head of Christendom.

In this respect he also differed from his royal colleagues. Dapper Francis I always fought for the political interests of France alone, and Henry pursued a very narrow but very realistic policy to assure economic advantages for himself.

It is the tragic fate of Charles that he not only differed from secular kings but even from most of the pontiffs of his time. He was more Christian, more Catholic, more religious than most of them, and, in his own way, guarded the welfare of Christendom more zealously than they did. His contemporaries on the throne of Peter were no credit to that high office. That is as true of the infamous war-minded Julius II as of the incapable Clement VII who became involved in the matrimonial tangles of the British monarch, lived through the sack of Rome, and was always motivated by his fear of the emperor whom he hated, rather than by Christian and papal principles.

The one exception among the popes was Hadrian VI, a high-minded, pious Hollander, who never became used to the atmosphere that prevailed at the curia during the Renaissance period. The Italians detested him as a foreigner, and the worldly Renaissance cardinals obstructed his administration so successfully that it became virtually ineffective.

The opposition to the Reformation was conducted by the emperor. He initiated every move from Worms to Augsburg and everything that happened between these two events. In all this the papacy assumed no leadership at all. But the whole life of Charles V was beset by tragedy. The only one of the three leading sovereigns of his generation who had lofty ideals and desired sincerely to serve the cause of Christianity and Europe, had failed. A broken man, he retired in 1556 to the monastery at San Yuste. In the words of an authority on the life of Charles "a great but futile life work had come to an end."

When he appeared for the last time before the assembled rulers at Brussels to announce his resignation, he had to lean for support on the shoulders of the young prince of Orange Nassau. The gesture was deeply symbolic, for the house of Nassau succeeded the Habsburgs and with the change came a new era of political and religious freedom.

For one brief moment the old and the new, the vanishing and the rising epoch, had touched each other. While the others with their unprincipled opportunism laid the foundations for the great national empires of France and Britain, the exalted vision of Charles was discarded. The time for his ideal of a European commonwealth was over. It is the bitter tragedy of history that it does not always reward the good and destroy the wicked.

Charles V is such a pathetic figure because he applied his great ability to achieve a goal that was no longer attainable.

It belonged hopelessly to the past. He fought for a Europe that was to be united in political structure as well as in religious faith. But the disintegration had set in too long before, and even his dogged and consecrated efforts could not rebuild what was already in ruins. This disintegration attacked the political structure first. For centuries, ever since there had been a western civilization, the empire had been the decisive political power. Not only Germany itself but Bohemia, Italy, the Netherlands, and Denmark had been part of it.

The main problem of the emperor had always been his relationship with these various ethnic groups. Under weak emperors the particularism of these nationalities had often assumed dangerous proportions. Yet nobody had seriously attempted to discredit the idea of the empire itself, though powerful princes had occasionally rebelled against it.

A new form of political organization came to the fore in the centuries that preceded the Reformation. At first it operated within the framework of the empire and had no relation to the main issues of empire policy. But in the fifteenth century it blossomed out and reached its state of perfection in the powerful city republics of Renaissance Italy. Such new structures are never the result of chance but of deeper reasons. As we inquire into them, we discover two distinct trends.

The first was the rise of the city itself. Since the middle of the thirteenth century the appearance of the European countryside had undergone profound changes. The towns had sprung up and a new sociological type of man inhabited them; the city dweller became important as he rose above the always suppressed peasants. "City atmosphere makes free." The new attitude soon expressed itself in a new community spirit and called for new administrative processes. The other factor was the new economic order which was brought about by the city itself. As the sixteenth century opened, the cities could already look back upon a long history. The free citizens felt themselves as important political factors, and the emperors found it frequently to their advantage to side with the often very powerful city dwellers against the princes of the territory.

Italy offered these city states the best opportunities for the development of their unique political genius. The Italians were the first people to experience a sense of national consciousness and develop political instruments for the expression of this feeling as a nation. Everyone knows the importance of Dante in this connection. The *Divine Comedy* combines devotion to the medieval Christian empire with a strong sense of Italian nationalism, to which Dante gave its first literary utterance.

Under the leadership of powerful patrician families the Italian city republics came into existence and were, as Burckhardt has accurately and minutely described them, the prototypes of the modern secular power state. Like a precious fruit in the sinking afternoon sun appears Venice, the queen of the seas. Her contacts reached deep into the East. So firmly and ably was she administered that she ranked among the great political and commercial powers of her day. With her wealth and her might, Venice became the most perfect expression of the Renaissance civilization. The first years of the sixteenth century cast the first dark shadows over all this loveliness; such fruits are always most luscious just before they fall. But in one respect Venice remained a leader for centuries: it had the most highly developed science of government and diplomacy. The Venetian ambassadors at the various courts of Europe were not only very shrewd observers but past-masters in the art of influencing the political moves of others. Their dispatches constitute to this day one of the most important sources of historical information about this period. In these city states the new doctrines were first formulated and expressed. The most famous of these declarations is, of course, Machiavelli's *The Prince.* One is amazed how clearly and realistically this man grasped the dynamics of the modern power state. He stated them with cool detachment, very soberly and logically, with complete indifference towards the traditional concept of the Christian state and its purposes.

So widely did these influences travel that we discover their traces in still another quarter. Thomas Aquinas, the great systematic theologian of the Catholic Church, had presented his concept of a Christian social order two centuries earlier. His blueprint for this ideal society, the *societas perfecta* is derived from the actually existing Italian city republics. But Thomas could not foresee the day when these theories would burst their narrow, easily controllable confines and form the basis for sovereign national states, thereby posing grave new questions for the Christian conscience.

It is a noteworthy fact that the secular political theories of Machiavelli, formed two hundred years after Thomas, displayed far greater vitality during the period of transition than the political philosophy of the great scholastic.

None of the lucidity, the genius for political leadership of the Italians, is found among the men who now make their entrance upon the stage of history, the princes. All their moves appear far less carefully planned and executed, and thereby seem clumsy in comparison. But by the time the sixteenth century dawns, the national state is definitely on its way. Its development required centuries, and it cannot surprise us that some of those who participated actively in its rise were not always conscious of the full implications of what they were doing.

Italy could not lead in the trend towards the creation of

national states, for its own independent republics prevented the unification of Italy. Many brilliant minds recognized this, and no one more clearly than the very un-popelike pontiff, Julius II. To unite Italy was the task to which he had dedicated himself, and it constantly involved him in military adventures which had no relation to his ecclesiastical office. Suffice it to say, that this man, who fought harder than any other Italian of his day for the unification of his native land, showed a very clear insight into a great historical and political necessity.

Where Italy failed, France and Britain were at least able to make a start. Their rulers, though they were not clearly aware of it themselves, laid the foundations for the greatness of their countries and their evolution into modern national states. What Francis had begun, Henry IV continued, but it was not completed until the days of Cardinal Richelieu and Louis XIV.

Henry's first stumbling attempts enabled Cromwell and Elizabeth afterward to establish England as a world power. The beginnings had been made for them, and they were important beginnings. It goes without saying that the German territorial princes likewise felt the impact of these new trends. They had their faults but they kept faith with the empire. How deep their loyalty was is clearly demonstrated by the fact that "The Holy Roman Empire of the German Nation" lasted until 1806 when it finally died of general debility. Regardless of its inherent weaknesses, the concept of the empire served as an element of cohesion until it became impossible to preserve it any longer. But it delayed Germany's unification long after the pattern of national states had been generally established throughout Europe. A federated *Reich* did not emerge until Prussia had become a modern state, and by that time France, England, and the Netherlands had long since completed their own evolution into national sovereign states.

One can readily perceive that the great political crisis of Europe developed independently of the Reformation. Its causes were the rise of nationalism, the diminishing prestige of the empire, the collapse of European unity, and the appearance of new political systems. It is not the fault of the Reformation that Europe ceased to be unified. This break up was not only "political" in a narrow sense but had far-reaching metaphysical consequences.

The medieval concept of the empire rested upon the parallelism of spiritual and temporal powers. Emperor and pope belonged together like sun and moon. Who was sun and who was moon often caused great differences of opinion, but the fact was never denied that they formed one team. Some secularistic historians of the late nineteenth century have claimed that the emperors never paid much attention to the popes and looked upon the church as a negligible factor. That is not only inaccurate history but a very inept projection of modern ideas into the minds of medieval men. The close relationship between emperor and pope, no matter who happened to be in control at the moment, symbolized the complete harmony of the medieval world order. The empire, as the highest sovereign power, assumed metaphysical proportions. The office of the emperor was divine in character and that fact constituted its dignity and authority.

As the medieval period drew to a close, rifts began to appear in this time-honored system. Papacy and empire began to drift apart and the process threatened to deprive the crown of its metaphysical importance. A comparison will show what the loss involved.

The great supernatural-political system which held the world together declined with the defeat of the Stauffen dynasty.[2] But by the "victory" over the emperor, the popes themselves initiated the trend which deprived the papacy of its universal appeal. It became steadily more Latin in character. At Avignon the College of Cardinals was controlled by French influences, and later members of the curia acted almost like Italian territorial princes. Opposition to the "foreign" papacy was bound to become an undercurrent in German life. But even the fact that some of these fifteenth-century popes were men of very dubious character did not seriously affect the combination of spiritual and temporal powers. The consciousness that they belonged together was too deeply rooted in the medieval mind. But when a new wave of unworthy popes occupied the throne of Peter in the early years of the sixteenth century, the effect was vastly different.

Those popes, for one thing, made it easy for the emperors to dominate them. Unknowingly, they helped to drive a wedge between the traditional allies. It was always a temptation for the pope to counteract the supremacy of the emperor by supporting his opponents. But as the rift between popes and emperors widened, the secular powers were inclined to drift further from their spiritual moorings. One can observe the final outcome of this process in such a character as Henry VIII. He is ultimately nothing but the manager of a business enterprise called England, and he operates it as though it were his private property. A tyrannical ruler can maintain this attitude for some time; but one of his successors paid

---

[2] Emperor Henry IV had to submit to the most humiliating conditions at Canossa (1077) in order to obtain release from the papal ban which would have discharged his subjects from their oath of allegiance to the emperor. It constituted Pope Gregory VII great triumph over the empire.

Pope Innocent III (1160-1216) finally achieved recognition for his claim that all German emperors must receive their crown at the hands of the Roman pontiff. (Tr.)

with his head for the loss of spiritual prestige which the crown had suffered.

The effects of all this can clearly be seen in the problems which beset the next decades and centuries. They concern the divine right of kings. These discussions merit our close attention. Machiavelli's theme was now taken up by the theologians. Bucer wrote a tract: *De rege et regimine*. Paradoxically he dedicated it to the heir presumptive of England, who at that time was still a well-meaning young prince. But it was already evident that the temporal authority no longer fitted readily into the metaphysical view of life. Its place in the scheme of things had now become a problem. Two centuries later a completely secularized absolutism stepped into this heritage.

The change in the political situation reveals itself even more drastically in the fortune of another, once mighty estate —the knights. Their fate is really a little pathetic, for this romantic element in medieval society simply vanished. There was no longer any place for it in the new society. Before chivalry disappeared altogether, it still blossomed in such figures as Georg von Frundsberg, dapper captain of his band of mercenaries, and Bayard, famed knight "without fear or blemish." But even they were affected by the new spirit. Georg's fame already rested on his reputation as a military strategist and Bayard dared to be saved without the intercession of Rome or the popes. Franz von Sickingen and Ulrich von Hutten were already relics of an age that had passed. Sickingen's frantic appeals found no response because no one was left to respond to them. Hutten symbolized the end of all knighthood by embracing the most modern of all professions—journalism with all its attendant virtues and evils.

What remained of chivalry was reduced to privileges; the real rights were gone. Knighthood finally succumbed not so much to a changed ideology as to a shift in social and economic values. The most potent factor was the transformation of the economic order which came as the result of the increased use of currency and the establishment of financial institutions. From the end of the fifteenth century the feudal lords had to face the embarrassing fact that land ownership was no longer a profitable form of wealth. Real estate found a serious competitor in capital which represented a more flexible type of property. The most disastrous effects of the new capitalistic order were not felt until the second half of the sixteenth century when the influx of Spanish gold and other precious metals caused serious economic dislocation.

As the new order began to reshape the economic life of Europe, bringing in its wake severe crises and disturbances, the knights lost their standing altogether, and their place was taken by their more fortunate competitors, the cities.

Behind these social forces, the old which receded and the new which were swept in, a new social group was forming. Its outlines were at first indistinct but gradually assumed recognizable forms and considerable drive—the people. For some time the movement appears chaotic. Now and then, for brief periods, one can distinguish an indisputable national consciousness, but it soon loses itself in the universalistic, medieval world view.

At the Council of Constance (1415) the delegates were arranged according to "nations" to counteract the preponderance of Italians, but this kind of nationalism is, of course, a far cry from the nationalism of the nineteenth century. During the controversy over the Hussite heresy, the Germans in Prague voted with the Czechs, just as the dissident Bohemians supported the German party. Nobody saw any inconsistency in the fact that German mercenaries, particularly the highly valued cavalry and foot soldiers, fought on opposite sides in the service of any ruler who cared to hire them. If Francis I and Henry VIII announced themselves as candidates for the German imperial throne, people only considered it ridiculous and brazen because they were obnoxious individuals. Their foreign background and nationality did not seem to create a serious impediment. Though all this belonged to the order of the day, there were occasional sudden and mighty upsurges of national feeling. It happened when the Italians ridiculed the devout Hadrian VII for his piety (an intolerable indignity to a pope) and harassed him simply because he was not an Italian. German national pride, this time more seemingly and spontaneously, rose to new heights when the celebrated humanist Erasmus passed through Germany on his way to Basle. Erasmus himself was overwhelmed by these enthusiastic ovations, the greatest and most cordial he had ever received. They were the more amazing because personally he preferred the centers of humanist learning at Paris and Oxford. Did his German admirers feel intuitively that Erasmus was merely a living symbol for their own sense of national dignity? He was capable of arousing this sense in others but he could never feel it himself. The true national genius was yet to arise: Luther on the way to Worms.

At this time antiquarians rediscovered the sources of German history. Scholars took Tacitus at his word when he described the high level of morality among the ancient Germans in his *Germania*. Wimpfeling wrote a new *Germania* which was almost chauvinistic. Deep forces of history were here at work and they were infinitely more valuable than the dynastic wars with their intrigues and ceaseless bloodshed.

Still another form of awakening took place during these years. It occurred in the world of faith and it was more than a beginning. Before we can discuss it, we must glance briefly at the intellectual life of the times.

A Changing World

If one reviews the broad expanse of the cultural and political life of the epoch, one feels the inadequacy of the usual question: Was a richly flourishing civilization rudely disturbed by the Reformation, or was Luther's work like a refreshing thunderstorm that cleared the air of impurities? The actual facts are both more simple and more complicated. The first decades of the sixteenth century belong at any rate to those periods in history which Goethe has characterized as "world-shaking transitions."

Man's ideas of the dimensions of the world underwent unprecedented changes. Columbus and his discoveries opened the eyes of his contemporaries to an entirely new mental picture of the globe.

This young, imaginative Genoese, who could find no encouragement for his undertakings at home and finally obtained the sloop "Santa Maria" from the queen of Spain, was an amazing character. A modern, almost Faustlike longing for far-away places was coupled with a profoundly medieval mysticism, an apt symbol for the merging of two epochs. He had been stimulated by reading a geography text by Pierre d'Ailly, a famous scholastic theologian at the University of Paris who had also influenced Luther's thinking. A book of meditations by the same author accompanied him on that adventurous expedition to East India which brought him to the West Indies. This book itself is a beautiful, deeply felt treatise by the very man who was largely responsible for sending John Huss to his death. Columbus represented in his own life the many lines that lead from the Middle Ages to the modern era. His discoveries compelled men to change their notions about the surface of the globe almost overnight. As a devout Catholic, Columbus gave Christian names to the places he discovered and his successors preserved this pious practice: Corpus Christi, San Salvador, Santa Maria de la Conception, and others. But beneath the thin veil of Christianity the ugliest and most cruel practices of colonization appeared immediately. The conquistadors came in droves. They no longer even pretended, as did the early crusaders, that they had come in the service of a supernatural religion which had enlightened Europe. They came as outright ruthless conquerors, and the first colonies witnessed the first outrages of colonialism.

Money became plentiful. The influx of gold and silver, which reached dizzy heights in the sixteenth century, made Spain the most prosperous nation and brought with it the eternal curse of gold. Spain could bear so much prosperity for only the span of one century, and all Europe was drawn into a spiral of economic crises which constantly increased in severity.

The world had become larger and its contours were better understood. Distant horizons appeared but they no longer frightened man or over-awed him. Just as he looked realistically at the West, he reappraised his eastern boundaries. The northern coast of Africa and the eastern Mediterranean became theaters of war in defense against the increasingly aggressive Turks. Some of the great victories in this struggle encouraged men in their belief that they were still masters of their world.

All this happened in a medieval atmosphere. The Inquisition flourished in Spain and spared not even Ignatius Loyola. Mystics and suppliants filled the world, and Columbus was one of them. Superstition of every kind reigned supreme and finally even claimed Columbus who ended his days in a Spanish prison cell. Once more man had reached out to the very limits of the known world. The spirit of expansion which had been dormant since the age of the Crusades awakened to new life. The Faustian age dawned and a Faust-like restlessness took hold of the minds of men. Astrologers sought new ideas, inventors appeared on the scene, everything was still in its early stages but destined to effect a fundamental change in man's view of the world. Man's fantasy traveled to the very edge of the world and the interest shifted to the distant lands in the West. The medieval world was almost as rigidly limited as the world of antiquity. It was organized around the Mediterranean. The first momentous step to break through these limitations had occurred.

Protestantism was the second step. It removed the Germanic nations from the homogeneous culture that had grown up in the Mediterranean basin. This is the external (one could almost say, geographical) proof of the end of the Middle Ages.

One sees it plainly in the changing political fortunes of Venice. The city was a unique political organism, one of the first modern states, an impressive achievement in the early sixteenth century. Its highly organized administration, its brilliant diplomacy, its superb combination of art and politics, its system of public representation, its fabulous wealth, its cuture, its affirmation of life, its comforts and refinements could only survive as long as the Mediterranean was the center of culture. As soon as geography, politics, and economics were viewed in terms of oceans, this splendor faded and Venice became what it is today—a resplendent museum.

The new geography was accepted with amazing swiftness and as a matter of course. There are always a few courageous and farsighted individuals who will take the first steps in a new direction. The masses soon learn how to trail behind and seek their own advantage under changed circumstances. The conquistadors streamed into the New World and their greed brought disaster to the guileless and ordinarily peaceful peoples and cultures with which they came in contact. Let it be remembered, however, that these devastators did not come alone. The messengers of Christ entered likewise into the New World. Dominican friars followed the plunderers and the noblest among them performed outstanding acts of piety and true humanity. One of the heroic figures in the early history of Christian missions is the Basque, Francis Xavier, the intimate of Ignatius Loyola. He began his missionary work in Goa in southern India, whence he had gone at the behest of the king of Portugal. A brilliant and restless mind, he pushed on when he conceived the, to our mind, almost fantastic plan to convert the imperial family of Japan. His impatience drove him farther. He died, literally at the gates of China, on a tiny island in the Yellow Sea. He was a remarkable example of the new spirit. A yearning for distant shores was coupled with a staunch faith in the medieval church.

The common, modern objection that the Christian faith alienates primitive peoples from their own culture, and that they would be happier in their own religion, never entered the minds of these early missionaries. The conquistadors never hesitated to force the Spanish way of life upon the natives. Modern liberals likewise impose "a technological civilization" and its "achievements" upon the peoples of the East, and never stop to inquire whether backward peoples really desire these "blessings" by which they become the victims of the industrial civilization of the West.

It is equally naive to raise the question whether the early missionaries were conscious of any violation of the rights of primitive man. The question itself would have been unintelligible to those ambassadors of Christ. Though their ideas about the physical nature of the world had undergone profound changes, the world of their faith had remained intact.

To the question why the Protestants did not participate in these early missionary efforts, the answer can readily be given: they had no opportunity. Protestantism developed under the protection of the German territorial princes who had no colonial possessions. As soon as Protestant powers acquired colonies, Protestantism organized its missionary program.

The new age advanced steadily. One of its most outstanding representatives is Erasmus, the prince of the humanists. A blond Hollander of medium height, with a delicate skin, a florid complexion and the finely formed features of the scholar, he was unquestionably the noblest and most mature figure among the humanists. He had risen above the slavish imitation of the ancient writers and had made Latin once more a living language. His collection of ancient proverbs, the *Adagia* proved to be a "best seller." Would-be literati found it a useful introduction to ancient civilizations, and his *Colloquies* were masterpieces of a refined, high-class type of journalism. They were the equivalent of the editorials in modern newspapers. If they were far more influential, we must remember that they had not yet become hackneyed attempts to sway public opinion, and that they owed their effectiveness to the superior quality of the work.

One is amazed at the freedom with which Erasmus attacked all forms of medievalism, including the practices of the church, though he always thought of himself as a faithful son of the church. Relics and pilgrimages were treated with such condescending but deadly irony that, on the surface, not even Luther's criticisms appear more caustic. In order to make Christian beliefs acceptable to his contemporaries, he incorporated so much of the new philosophy into the traditional dogma that the tight system of medieval theology was punctured in many places. In one of his Oxford "conversations" he relates the story of the angel who guards Paradise with a drawn sword. A character in the dialogue addresses the angel: "Hey, you, what are you standing around for with this silly gadget? Are you still patrolling the garden? Nowadays people use dogs for jobs like that." He continues by connecting the myth of Prometheus who rebelled against the gods with the biblical story of the fall of man; it is done in such a clever manner that the fundamental differences become obliterated. It is typical, a blinding twilight that characterizes this whole period. "The intellectual heaven is reorganized," as Burckhardt expressed it.

The most sensitive gauge of the spiritual life, art, proves it. The beautiful golden background, which transfigured the pictures of the saints in the cathedral of Sienna and elevated them above common humanity, disappeared. Gentle bluish landscapes and sweeping views over rivers and valleys took their places. The human form lost the hieratic stiffness of the liturgical pictures. Garments appear draped, the facial expression becomes alive; real human beings emerge. Sculpture shows the trend even more clearly. Real figures of flesh and blood step out of the shadowed arches and pillars of the Gothic cathedrals. Sculptors had represented the saints as elongated figures, delicate in their otherworldliness, in ecstatic gestures of prayer. These works of art harmonized perfectly with the bewildering array of rising arches and flying buttresses which constitute the unique beauty of the Gothic cathedral. But they had to make room for the perfectly proportioned, lifelike representation of the human form which the sculptors had learned from the study of the ancient masterworks.

Here likewise was not a gradual change from one period to another but a struggle between conflicting forces. The old world did not merely retreat before the new; the two clashed and both currents finally merged like the flood waters of two mighty rivers. Hieronymous Bosch provides a good illustration. At the turn of the century he painted the "Garden of Passions." A multitude of demons are released by human desires; phantom-like figures fill the picture. All evil spirits are let loose. An ear that had listened only to music is pierced by the needle pricks of never ending music. A small human figure is welded to a harp. Gambling, hunting, lust, and gluttony are represented. But in the midst of this thoroughly medieval portrayal of evil, we notice a pale human countenance, medieval in appearance and horrified by this pandemonium. In reality it is an altogether modern face, human and very familiar in its awareness of life. It is a man, a real human being in a world of medieval fantasies.

It is amazing and significant that these developments appear side by side. Grünewald finds his successor in Dürer, Breughel takes the place of Bosch. The transition appears to have been particularly even in the field of music. Some of the great melodies of the Middle Ages live on and a new age fills them with new content and sings them with new fervor, particularly Luther's majestic "In the midst of life, we are in death" (*Mitten wir im Leben sind mit dem Tod umgeben*). In the rewriting of the medieval *Media vita in morte sumus,* the new understanding of the faith, which separates the Middle Ages from the new era, finds powerful and effective expression. One obvious explanation for the triumph of the new philosophy was the invention of the printing press. The business of publishing and marketing books was, of course, still in its infancy. Printers were also publishers and printed any material they could find or that was offered to them. There were no copyright laws, and no author was protected against plagiarism. Very few people could see any unfairness or dishonesty in such a state of affairs. Luther, probably the most prolific writer of his age, never derived any income from his books, though his printer sold enough copies to build a very substantial home in Wittenberg from the sale of Luther's writings. The printed word had a tremendous effect on the reading public. For the first time the circulars, books, and pamphlets created what is now known as "public opinion." The almost unbelievable popularity of Erasmus depended solely upon the existence of the printing press. Only by its use could he hope to popularize the wisdom of the ancients and make his voice heard in the religious controversy. He always recognized that Gutenberg's invention, which enabled the leaders of thought to influence the rank and file, was the greatest single step toward progress in his day. He must have felt like the men who at a later date discovered the almost limitless propaganda possibilities of the radio.

The Erasmian ideal depended upon the printing press. In one of his loveliest, most often quoted statements, Erasmus spoke of his wish to place a copy of the New Testament in the hands of even the most common man. Such an ideal was only attainable when the ownership of a Bible no longer required a large financial investment because the book could be produced at moderate cost on the printing presses.

Not only in matters of faith but in all other aspects of life—politics and economics—was it important that a public opinion existed. Though it was politically still impotent, it could at least exercise some control. Three more centuries had to pass before the people could participate actively in the decisions which intimately affected their personal destinies. But in matters of the spirit, which were then, as now, important factors, it had already become inadvisable to ignore public sentiments, and popes and princes were soon to learn it. It is impossible to think of the Reformation without this most modern instrument for the dissemination of spiritual knowledge.

The populous towns were the ideal soil for the growth of public opinion. In religious as in civic matters it was proven again: city air makes free. It is no coincidence that the leaders in the Protestant movement were the free imperial cities. They were strong enough to form opinions of their own and stand by them. Luther was the first man to make full use of the new invention. Only through the printer's art was it possible that public opinion came almost exclusively under the influence of one man.

The Church

Another, and in many respects the most potent force in the Middle Ages, was the church. She presented an imposing outward appearance. She was visibly represented by the pope, and never had this visible evidence of her reality been more impressive. It is an amazing panorama of individual popes who pass before our eyes. Before we can understand them as individuals, we must look at the status of the papacy itself.

Ever since the middle of the fifteenth century the popes had conducted themselves almost like territorial princes. Rome had become intoxicated with the splendor of the Renaissance. A spirit of worldliness, nurtured on the classical ideal of beauty, prevailed at the curia, the courts, and throughout public life. The moving elements of this new freedom were, however, not only poets, sculptors, painters, and architects, but unfortunately as often poison, lewdness, murder, and lust for power. One is constantly startled by the apparent unconcern with which the Renaissance popes accepted this situation as normal. One of the very worst popes inspired the creation of the Sistine Chapel, thus acquiring a double reputation as a patron of the fine arts and an arch villain. This self-assurance reached such proportions that it almost impresses one by its sheer boldness and audacity. Alexander VI Borgia, the last of this line of corrupt Renaissance popes, liked to appear on the balcony of the papal palace, his arm thrown around his daughter, to view the thoroughbreds in the papal stables. Here is an unregenerate man, strong and handsome, hard and cunning, a true scion of the family of robber barons from whom he was descended. Recent researches make it almost certain that he died of a dose of poison he had intended for somebody else. Even the passion for revenge was unrestrained in this vicar of Christ.

A very similar person reigned on the throne of Peter in the early years of the sixteenth century. Adopting a suggestion by Erasmus, Luther always referred to Julius II as "blood-bibber" (*Blutsaeufer*). We know from a pamphlet published at that time that the age was outraged by the cruel wars which the pope personally directed. A spirited humanistic dialogue, *Julius exclusus,* depicts the pope in his official vestments, worn over the blood-stained armor, at the heavenly gate. He is denied admission because St. Peter will not tolerate such a tainted soul in heaven. In fairness one must state that Julius II, like Machiavelli, recognized Italy's weakness as the result of its territorial particularism and, applying the famous formula of a later statesman (Bismarck), tried to rectify the situation by "blood and iron." Such projects do credit to Julius' political acumen, but they certainly went far beyond the duties which his high Christian office demanded of him. His contemporaries, at any rate, were gravely offended by his seeming inability to distinguish between a helmet and the tiara, even though they were quite accustomed to war-minded princes.

This condemnation itself is an indication of the new public spirit. The disgraceful papal regime of an earlier century, with its poison deaths, adultery, and utter worldliness, had distressed no one but a few representatives of the "inner life," while the great majority of Christians remained indifferent. That was changed now.

The sixteenth century saw the end of the reign of the Borgias and the rise of the house of Medici, a family of bankers whose great wealth enabled them in time to rank with the reigning houses of Europe. Two women members of the family even ascended the throne of France in the sixteenth and seventeenth centuries. The Medici popes were men of refinement, charm, considerable ability, and political skill, though they were by no means uniformly successful. Leo X, who was pope at the time Luther published his ninety-five theses, would have liked nothing better than to dispose of the distasteful quarrel in Germany by a peaceful and magnanimous settlement. His cousin Giulio Medici, who served as his papal secretary of state and later became Pope Clement VII, inherited a difficult political situation. Finances were at a very low ebb, and he had the misfortune to become involved in the struggle between France and the Habsburgs and was almost annihilated. During his regime occurred the *sacco di Roma* (1527), when revolting mercenaries looted the city and despoiled it with unspeakable horror. It fell to his lot to render the final decision in the matrimonial troubles of Henry VIII. This was another agonizing obligation, for Henry used the decision as a pretext to separate the Church of England from Rome. Historians have probably given Clement too much credit when they praised him for his staunch adherence to ecclesiastical principles. The curia had been able to find loopholes in the canon law in more complicated cases, without feeling restrained by principles. The real reason was that in the game of power politics, Charles V, the nephew of the English queen, appeared more important than Henry. It just so happened that one incompetent pope was at the same time presented with the account for all the errors of his predecessors, who had long ignored the spirit and the real tasks of the papacy. Ranke and Pastor[1] have termed his pontificate the "most fateful" in the history of the papacy. His disloyalty and fickleness towards Charles gave the Protestant princes freedom of action. Clement caused untold damage by his quiet but determined opposition to the call of a general council of the church. Was he a bad pope? The very tendencies which appeared as marks of strength in Julius II had by now become glaring weaknesses. The papacy had turned itself into an undisguised political power state. But Italy, whose particularism Julius had been unable to overcome, was not the land for such political ambitions. The pope controlled too little territory to count as a sovereign secular ruler. Such a policy could only lead to a very modest role as a third-rate Italian territorial prince, a pawn in the hands of the great powers who contended for the domination of Italy. There was no way out, despite the many diplomatic moves—Ranke calls them intrigues—in which the popes were constantly engaged. It was said that the curia even gave serious thought to an alliance with the king of France and the Turks against the emperor.

The same predicament had beset Julius II. There was no solution to the political task he had chosen for himself. He either had to wear the tiara or the helmet but he could not wear both at the same time. If the papacy wished to remain influential, as it certainly did, it had to substitute political and diplomatic adroitness for the lack of outward territorial power. In time, the papacy became extraordinarily efficient in that respect. Though the pope had just been bitterly humiliated by Napoleon, his papal secretary, Consalvi, was able

---

[1] Ludwig von Pastor (1854-1928) Roman Catholic professor of history at the University of Innsbruck, wrote among other works a *History of the Popes since the Renaissance* in 16 vols. He was the first historian to whom the pertinent material in the Vatican archives was made available. (Tr.)

to play a role at the Congress of Vienna which was not inferior to that of Metternich and Talleyrand.

A lonely and strangely attractive figure among the Medici
and other Italian popes is the Hollander, Hadrian VI. He
appears like the harbinger of a new era, a better papacy. He
had been the tutor of Charles V. His imperial master had
entrusted him with important political missions in Spain and
finally secured the papal crown for him. But he was a strange
pontiff, everything but an Italian *capitano* or indulgent Renaissance noble. Here was a pope who introduced his statement to the Diet at Nuremberg in 1522-23 with a confession
of the church's guilt. He was a dangerous pope because he
was in such deadly earnest. One speculates whether the Reformation would ever have led to the break with Rome if this
faithful, consecrated man had been at the helm during the
decisive years of the conflict. But a pope who took the church
and his own office seriously was still an impossible figure in
Rome. The cardinals laughed at his Germanic honesty, the
courtiers ridiculed his artlessness, and the Italians despised
him because he could not speak their language. They had
no use for a pope who was not interested in the (for them)
primary task of solving the Italian territorial dilemma. An
early death released Hadrian from a bitter and hopeless fate.
The beautiful monument in the Church of Santa Maria
dell'Anima in Rome epitomizes his noble but futile career
in one symbolic gesture: his left hand supports his dying head
for which the papal crown has become too heavy. The
policy of the Medici was resumed once more. Hadrian's papacy remained an episode, but it proved conclusively that
one could not look to Rome for a renewal of the church.
Hadrian had been unable to change anything. He was not
even understood in a society whose chief characteristic, in
Burckhardt's words, was a "magnificent joviality." It is in-

deed amazing that this festive and splendid world, and "world" it was, with its charm and grandeur, its harmony and stateliness could survive the wars and political confusion of the times. The restoration of the church could never have started here; it had to begin somewhere else. Ignatius Loyola, the stern Basque officer and mystic, was to become the general who reconquered Europe for the church. The popes could never have done it themselves.

If one dismisses the notion that popes and cardinals ought to be servants of Christ and his church, one can admit that they were distinguished and able men. When Julius II died at the age of seventy, still fired with ambition, he had completed a life of remarkable military and diplomatic achievements. He was a farsighted political leader, thoroughly realistic in his thinking and almost modern in his unconcern about his methods—but he was no pope. The princes of the church who had met a century before at Constance to pronounce judgment upon the Bohemian heretic John Huss used the days when the council was not in session to search the neighborhood for valuable documents and took precious scrolls from the monasteries at St. Gall, Reichenau, and Ufenau to Rome. It is well known how the arts flourished in those days. The very worst popes subsidized Michelangelo, Raphael, and countless other artists, and saw to it that their successors could live and work in palaces and cathedrals which are famous the world over. Anyone who could see a little deeper and learn something about the papal finances, and many contemporaries were able to do that, was almost bound to ask himself: how is it possible to revel in all this splendor and still claim to be a disciple of Him who on earth had not where to lay His head?

What little had remained of spiritual authority the popes themselves dissipated. As the arbitrariness with which they administered their spiritual prerogatives increased, people reacted with growing indifference to excommunications and interdicts. Even the simplest and most devout Christian must have been startled when he learned of the decree of Pius II that failure to buy salt from the papal mines at Tolta was a mortal sin for which one could not receive absolution. Excommunication and interdict had once been powerful spiritual disciplines. If the papacy itself brought them into disrepute, their effectiveness was at an end. It still fills one with dismay to see how hardened people had become. They accepted the deterioration of the papacy with stolid complacency. A "reform of head and members" was such an urgent and obvious necessity that no one even took the trouble to defend the existing conditions.

Equally severe was the loss of prestige which the monastic orders had suffered. At one time they had been the most courageous, unselfish, and successful defenders of the church. Most seriously affected were the mendicant orders. In the thirteenth century they had almost revitalized the church and rendered invaluable service when the rise of the towns and mass migrations presented new tasks to the church. But poverty, which had been preached by St. Francis, had degenerated into beggary and beggary into indolence. The immorality of the Franciscans had become a byword; their lack of discipline and the crass stupidity of their canonists furnished Erasmus with ever new material for his brilliant, biting essays. The great mission to which the monastic orders had dedicated themselves since the days of Benedict of Nursia[2] seemed forgotten, and the pious and sincere men and women who could still be found behind the cloister walls remained

---

[2] Author of the *Regula S. Benedictini* which became the basic rule for occidental monasticism. Little is known of his life; between A.D. 529 and 542 he established the famous monastery at Monte Cassino, which became the first Benedictine monastery. (Tr.)

hidden from the eyes of the world. What the public did see were all too often the frauds and charlatans.

There were, however, other manifestations of the religious life. It is touching to observe how the people reached out for them; the piety of the little people longed for something to sustain them. Much of it can only be described as a mechanization of religion that ended frequently in sheer superstition. The magical element, the relics, indulgences, pilgrimages took an ever firmer hold. One can read about them in the *Colloquies* of Erasmus, where he subjects these practices to an objective, brilliant, yet not irreligious criticism. But the cultured essays of the humanists prevailed little against a fact more powerful than logic: the dreadful fear that medieval man had of death, purgatory, and the torments of hell. This world, in which man had to die, was his world. The never-ceasing wars claimed not only the lives of soldiers but the inhabitants of whole territories as well. Men were helpless against the virulent epidemics which broke out time and again in the unsanitary, overcrowded cities. *Media vita in morte sumus* was as real as the daily bread, unless one belonged to the social or intellectual elite who could always flee from an epidemic-stricken community.

No other writers were, therefore, as influential as the men who could offer comfort in the face of death. One of the finest products of its kind is the precious little book by a truly pious soul, Thomas á Kempis, *De Imitatione Christi.* Here, amidst the clamor of the papal court and the learned but ultimately vague pronouncements of the humanists, the still small voice is heard by which the exalted Lord directs his followers. It is like a soothing melody which helps to forget the noise of all the others. Luther thought very highly of this little book which had become the Bible of the people. Its fundamental teachings and basic outlook can be found in other writings. In the rich symphony of medieval life we detect again and again the strain of praise and adoration through which those who truly sought God extolled their Lord. The splendor of kings and prelates predominates and gives color to the scene, but this adoration of God was never completely missing.

In order to round out this picture of the intellectual civilization of the Middle Ages, we must briefly consider its achievements in the field of theology. The spirit of the age found its most characteristic expression in theological scholarship, and created its own style which corresponded to the subject matter. The great systems, which encompass the total knowledge of the Middle Ages, are worthy counterparts of the great cathedrals. What the Gothic style meant for architecture, scholasticism meant for theology and all occidental civilization. That has been stated so often that it should be generally understood. If there are still people who fail to appreciate this intellectual achievement, they do so because they judge it by the standards of an already outdated liberalism.

But regardless of this emotional prejudice against medieval theology, it is not easy to present a brief account which will be intelligible to the nontheological reader. We can best begin the task by an examination of the final phases of medieval theological thought.

The foundation had been laid by Thomas Aquinas. All of his great works bear the title *summa* and they are, indeed, summaries of the total knowledge of the times. The arrangement of this vast amount of material alone represents an intellectual achievement of the first order. But Thomas was more than a cataloguer. He was able to give a Christian interpretation of the new world view that came as a result of the rediscovery of Aristotle. The most revolutionary effects of the advance of the Arabs into the West had been in the realm of the spirit. A great deal of Greek literature that had been lost in the West had been preserved among the Arabs. It was through them that the vanished world of the Greeks, their philosophy and science, their mathematics and astronomy, came to light once more. Christianity was called upon to examine this new knowledge thoroughly and come to terms with it. That became the gigantic task of scholastic theology and no one did it more painstakingly and, therefore, effectively than Thomas Aquinas. His clear logic and closely knit argumentation formed the basis for all future intellectual and theological inquiries and his successors for centuries depended upon the methods of Thomas.

The reader who knows something of the great importance of Thomism for modern Catholicism will notice an amazing development. Ever since Leo XIII declared St. Thomas a *doctor ecclesiae* and made Catholic dogmatics dependent upon his system, Thomistic thought in the form of Neo-Thomism has reigned supreme in Catholic theology. This theology is frequently little more than a commentary on St. Thomas. Even distinguished Catholic thinkers of undisputed scholarship and personal piety submit to the ultimate authority of the great Scholastic. A particular problem is subjected to an often keen and searching analysis and then reduced to general principles, which slip easily and gracefully into the framework of Thomistic theology. It may seem paradoxical that the Middle Ages enjoyed a much greater independence. For one thing, St. Thomas had not yet risen to the position as final arbiter, which the decree of Leo XIII bestowed upon him. Another and more important factor was the fluidity which still characterized the development of scholastic thought.

Two Anglo-Saxons, Duns Scotus and William Occam,

expressed their dissatisfaction with the tightly closed meta-physical system of the Italian nobleman. A breath of modernity pervades their thought. Thomas had assumed that the Christian faith furnished an answer to every possible question, and that the harmony between faith and reason assured the validity of his system for all times. The new theologians were far more skeptical with regard to the capacity of human reason. We cannot claim that the concepts (*nomina*) we form always correspond to reality. We must accept this limitation which precludes full cognition of reality. That is particularly true when we speak of God. These Anglo-Saxon thinkers and their schools considered it a mark of man's deference for God's revelation to say no more about it than God had permitted us. This retrenchment and revision of Thomism agitated the century before the Reformation. Pierre d'Ailly and Johannes Gerson, the two outstanding representatives of this new line of thought were also the leading ecclesiastics at the Council of Constance. It is a sad fact that the council which condemned John Huss to death was guided by the advice of two eminent theologians who were among the most intelligent and progressive thinkers of their time. They reflected already the influence of that other great movement, humanism, which ended medieval theology. Its scope was wider than theology proper, but its most significant contributions were made in the field of religion. We must refer once more to Erasmus, because he most impressively represents the theological achievements of humanism. His real accomplishments have been too often obscured by his mistakes which are unduly emphasized. If one cannot forgive the fact that he was no Luther, one should at least remember that he was the most mature and most sincere among the humanists. He was motivated by a genuine yearning for purity, peace, and orderliness; this longing inspired the many activities by which he dominated the thinking of his age. His intelligent criticism of ecclesiastical abuses contributed materially to the success of the Reformation. He rendered a most valuable service by his theological studies, particularly the emendation of Christian texts, among which the New Testament of 1516 is the most important. This particular publication, unfortunately, reflects no credit upon Erasmus the scholar. It was prepared in inexcusable haste and with great carelessness. Erasmus himself admits that it was *praecipitatum magis quam editum* (more pushed out than edited).

But he prepared the ground for the Reformation as few others had done. What he had to say about the study of the Scriptures, their greatness, their significance for time and eternity, must be counted among the finest tributes to the Bible before Luther.

The value of the theology of this epoch was that it raised practically all the problems which were to find a solution in the Reformation. The great restlessness of the age is also reflected in its theology. The universal demand for a "reform in head and members" is represented here in the critical discussions about the papacy, the monastic ideal, the practice of indulgences. Almost all the questions had been asked. Christendom awaited the answers.

Summary

If one ponders these questions against the general background of the times, it becomes clear that the answers could come only from God. We mean primarily that such an event as the Reformation cannot be regarded as the work of a single individual. The questions whether Luther created or tore down, set free or laid waste, miss the point altogether. What happened here takes us into the inner sanctum of history, where men are no longer free agents, but instruments of a divine purpose that unfolds itself in the historical process. Only through such an approach are we placed in the position to render fair judgment. To start from any other premise must inevitably confuse the issue.

Only if one does violence to one's scientific conscience can one draw a portrait of the Middle Ages as the gifted Catholic historian Johnannes Janssen has done.[1] He simply narrowed his field of vision to the flowering of medieval piety, without

---

[1] Johannes Janssen (1829-91) Catholic priest and teacher of history at the Gymnasium in Frankfort am Main, was a romanticist with strong nationalistic German leanings and dislike for everything un-Germanic, particularly Renaissance art and Roman law. His chief contribution as historian is his interest in the "little man," the artisans, farmers, towns people, whom Ranke and his school of political historians had consistently ignored. Janssen's colorful *History of the German People* is a running attack upon the Reformation and the personal character of the Reformers. The fact that Luther sided with the princes against the "common people" and the introduction of the *Corpus Juris Romanum* into German life, by which the peasants could be exploited, accounts for the decline of a flourishing Catholic civilization and German political fortunes. (Tr.)

ever raising the crucial question of why men had become so restless in the late fifteenth century. Only oversimplification to the point of distortion can find the cause for the decline of this piety in the personal act of one individual, Martin Luther.

Equally misleading is the opposite view which is often hailed as genuine Protestantism: Luther had "liberated" men from medieval obscurantism and spiritual serfdom. Of course, in a certain sense, he did this, but certainly not as a forerunner of modern liberalism. It was liberalism which prided itself in the middle of the last century that it had brought freedom to men everywhere. It was this kind of liberalism which men traitorously scuttled in the twentieth century, in their piteous surrender to a new tyranny.

The true depths of these historical circumstances is rather to be seen in the following comments. Luther stands at one of the crossroads where the great figures in history most often appear in response to a deep inner necessity. Why it should be so remains an enigma without an outwardly satisfactory explanation. When these great personages appear, we soon realize that the next great step forward could not have been taken in any other manner. It was as at the time when the cities arose and the population increased in the thirteenth century, and the Dominicans and Franciscans came on the scene. They were able to give the services which a new situation demanded of the church, but which the papal regime of Innocent III, in spite of its splendor and its world-wide influence, could never have rendered by itself.

Luther stands at such a critical junction in history. He did not create the forces which form the background of events. They existed before him. This searching and brooding restlessness had entered the world before his time. The bewildering interplay of inventions and discoveries, of wars and revolutions, of political reorganizations and intellectual changes was already at work.

It remains one of the inexplicable mysteries of the divine Providence that Luther appeared at this moment and in this environment. Lagarde[2] who for complex personal reasons hated Luther said occasionally of Luther that he, like Bismarck, merely expressed the silent mood of the masses who supported him and carried him along, once he had become their spokesman. Actually, Luther—according to Lagarde—had as little originality as Bismarck. Malicious as the statement is, it contains a grain of truth. The world into which Luther was born contained the possibility of countless historical combinations. He became the one who was chosen to release the accumulated tensions. He loosened the avalanche. He was not the exponent of the masses (that is materialistic thinking), but the instrument of a divine purpose which placed him at this moment upon the stage of history.

All speculation as to what would have happened had Luther not appeared is, therefore, besides the point and futile. The fact is that he did appear. The Reformation had been due for a long time, and before that reality it becomes meaningless to figure out what other solutions might have been possible. One can almost prove this historically. The old world, particularly the sacred world of the church and the faith, was slowly disintegrating and nobody tried to arrest the process. That is the one fact which always surprises the student of the Reformation. The time had come, the historic hour of destiny had struck.

Luther's personal significance lies in the fact that he fought in his own soul the intellectual conflict which held the West-

---

[2] Paul Anton de Lagarde (real name Bötticher 1827-91), professor of oriental languages in Goettingen, one of the earliest advocates of a "national Germanic" religion. He opposed Catholicism, but approved the Catholic doctrine of the sacraments because they "symbolized" the presence of the divine on earth. He was bitter in his rejection of St. Augustine, Luther, and the "Pharisee" St. Paul. (Tr.)

ern world in its grip. Or more specifically: as he struggled on toward a new faith, he determined vicariously the course of Europe's future spiritual pilgrimage. How this vicarious struggle developed, and why we assign such decisive importance to it, will be shown later. That it had this importance no one can very well deny. In many aspects of life, even those only remotely related to faith, Western civilization accepted the decisions which were born of this spiritual agony. That is true, though many of these aspects have since reverted to the mundane. It is true even of the Catholic Church itself. The efforts to renew Catholicism by the decrees of the Council of Trent owe their inspiration to Luther. He has helped Catholicism to effect its own Reformation.

All these interactions disclose the real enigma of history. We have sketched this colorful, fascinating picture of the medieval world in order to emphasize the truly creative forces which came to the fore. How brilliant the portrait is—kings, emperors, popes, warriors, statesmen, diplomats, scholars! How modest the work and world of the Reformers appear alongside them! While the great rulers made decisions changing the map of Europe, the Reformers busied themselves with pamphlets, booklets, creeds, and confessions, obviously mere chaff before the strong winds of political realities.

And yet, what remains of the political decisions which these rulers sought on the blood-drenched battlefields of their never-ceasing warfare?

Neither dialectical materialism, nor worse yet, shallow superficiality, can obliterate the fact that the theology of the Reformers has affected successive centuries more deeply than any political, intellectual, or economic factor. Even the greatest of the external events appear like debris which covers the battlefields of history. Beneath it are the real forces which determined—and still determine—the course of events.

<u>Part II</u>

The Work

The Reformation is more than Martin Luther. And the sixteenth century—this watershed of modern history—is more than the Reformation. Why then is it that Luther's figure stands forth so commandingly in the foreground?

There can be pointed out at once an external reason for this: he stands at the beginning, he is the start of the great work. This lifts him out of the line of the truly great and significant figures with which the outbreak of the Reformation is blessed. Of course, Zwingli came to his ideas of reformation without Luther, but then he opened himself wide to Luther's influence even though he did not accept everything he found there. The others are not even to be thought of without Luther: Bucer, Blaurer, Bugenhagen—not even Melanchthon, the greatest single individual and by far the finest mind of the Reformation, who was both Luther's warm friend and devoted follower—nor even Calvin whose great systematic and organizational gifts were to push the work of the Reformation into areas which Luther would never have reached. None of them would have called himself anything other than Luther's pupil.

But the question involves more than this historical precedence. There is a profoundly essential reason for Luther's standing out above the other reformers. This can be seen if the figures of the Reformation are compared from another angle. The great, dispassionate thinkers of humanism come first; as for example, Erasmus or Thomas Moore. But for all the sincerity of their thought and their objectives they remained intellectual aristocrats—even the fame of Erasmus in Europe was based on his scholarship. After these come the men of action: Calvin and Ignatius Loyola (who is mentioned only for the sake of clarity in the comparison). These are the great figures. The far-reaching effect of their lives' work is based on the fact that they gave historically effective form to the tasks it fell to them to perform.

It is quite apparent that Luther was neither one nor the other—neither just a philosopher nor just an organizer. But his life was the ground on which the basic conclusions of the Reformation were fought out. The foundation of the great work of the humanists and the beginnings of the work that Calvin carried on can be seen in the things Luther suffered through, prayed through, fought through, and achieved in faith. It cannot be said in any other way—Luther's struggle of faith has a representative meaning. He had neither a cultural program nor world-encircling organizational plans. He was simply himself, going his own path, fighting his way through the problems of faith that were laid upon him. If he was to perform the services for world and church history which were laid at his door, he could not have done it in any other way than by being just himself. This is why he is so personal; why it is impossible properly to appraise his work apart from the personal course of his life; and why he is at all times and in all things more lively and direct than the systematic thinkers and the organizers. There is no point in talking about weakness or greatness, limitations or importance; this personal path which he trod was his contribution to the Reformation—it was the medium of historical effectiveness. In this sense Luther was the tool of God in history.

For this reason it is unavoidable that we should examine his life, though not as psychologists who are interested primarily in an analysis of his character, nor as "hero-worshipers" who stand in awe before the personal greatness of this man. Let us rather look at the example and the meaning of his life as the place where historical decisions were made which were destined to determine not only the course of the Reformation but a whole epoch of Western history as well.

It cannot surprise us then that the life of Luther differed fundamentally from the lives of other great men of his time. Luther's world was vastly different from the world in which Francis I or Henry of England was at home. They and their associates lived a much wider life, but despite its dimensions they were always self-seeking. It was not even the welfare of their subjects that mattered; these crass egoists cared for no one but themselves. And many were the men in church and university circles who were sucked into the same whirlpool of personal ambition and greed for recognition. Luther differed basically from them all—for he was a man who suffered. He was not a daring fighter whom a romantic age loved to depict, he was not even a "hero" in the ordinary sense of the word. He was indeed a warrior in the sense that he struggled with God.

It is in this fight with death and devil that we see Luther as an example—that we see his vicarious significance. It was no intention of his that, in the course of his personal struggles, the fight should expand to world-wide importance and draw into itself all the forces of history and finally shake the foundation of Europe. Rather did it force itself upon him as the vehicle of God's will in history. Luther himself has best expressed this enigma of God's shaping of history in the drastic expression: "God had led me into all this 'like a blind nag.'"

This expression indicates a deep reverence for the *mysterium* of the divine will, and we would do well to recognize this hidden guidance as of greater importance than biographical details. Any other concept of Luther biography remains inadequate. This is especially true of any attempt to treat Luther in the manner of Carlyle's hero worship: to declare Luther as one of the great figures in history and then interpret the modern world in terms of his influence.

Luther stated emphatically and repeatedly[1] that he was fully aware of the fundamental difference between greatness, as the humanists understood it, and the divine call by which he had become the instrument of God's will. It was not simply modesty or the admission of an evident reality which induced him to take this position. He was both modest and realistic, and in that sense he was a great man; even a "genius." But what impressed Luther profoundly were the implications of the First Commandment: God's work is done by God—man is only the instrument.

To put it in the form of a paradox: there would have had to be a "Lutheran" church even if there had never been a Luther. The importance lies not in Luther but in the gospel, not in the historical admiration of a man, but in the presence of Christ.[2] It is only with this premise in mind that there is any value in looking into the significance of Luther and his work.

---

[1] The most pointed of these statements is in the Weimar edition of his works, VIII, p. 685.

[2] It is interesting that precisely those periods in the history of the church which produced something like a "cult of Luther" had very vague, superficial notions of Luther's church. The church must always be on guard against any attempts to make a hero of Luther. And this would have been Luther's own opinion.

Martin Luther

What we find in all other great figures in history is also present in Luther's case. The great and unique are mingled with the ordinary and commonplace. There are some individuals who seem already destined by their heredity and background to become leaders in the great world of affairs. Richelieu, scion of an aristocratic French family that had been traditionally associated with the Catholic Church, was such a person. Loyola, the Spanish nobleman and former army officer, seemed well prepared for his future role as a commander of men. Luther was not one of these. Actually, he came of peasant stock and belonged to that great mass of common people who still formed a vast untapped reservoir of strength. The peasants were known as the fourth estate. Poor as they were, they had not yet sunk to the level of destitution that one finds in the slum areas of our industrial centers. The proletarization of the masses is a sociological phenomenon that came later in the wake of a technological civilization. Luther's family had always shown a desire to improve their economic status. Father Hans Luther had originally been a coal miner. By determined effort and diligence he had acquired a business of his own and could plan to give his son a university education. Luther frequently mentioned the hardships of his childhood and the penurious habits of his father; they served him as excellent preparations for his later life. The father's moderate success in business and the comparative independence he was able to achieve bore fruit for the son. Martin was the first member of the Luther family to receive an academic education.

No event during the first two decades of his life pointed to any greatness or distinction in the future. The day following his birth, November 11, 1483, he was baptized in the church in Eisleben. Sixty-three years later in the same small town in Thuringia he was to die—the circle of his life completed after having shaken the world.

When the child was one year old, his father moved to Mansfeld. Luther began his education in the *Trivial* (elementary) school. He was taught the customary subjects— ecclesiastical Latin, spelling, music and a little arithmetic. Like many another great man, Luther did not cherish the memory of his schooldays but probably owed more to them than he realized. In 1497 he was sent to Magdeburg and entered the school of the Brothers of the Common Life. This brotherhood was the most genial of the semimonastic organizations. It had been a stronghold of a sincere lay piety and in all, likelihood, the fourteen-year-old youth was favorably impressed by it. We have, however, only one detail about his life in Magdeburg. A prince of Anhalt practiced the most severe type of asceticism by begging for his food in the streets. That made a great impression upon the boy Luther who remarked that anyone who saw him "just smacked his lips with devotion." The statement probably indicates little more than youthful enthusiasm. We can follow his development more closely as he transferred a year later to Eisenach. All his life he remembered Eisenach as "his good city" and the glow of happy student days seems to linger over the memories. Like many of his classmates he supported himself as a member of the *Kurrende*[1]. He was "discovered" by a fine, motherly

---

[1] A choral group whose members performed for the benefit of wealthy patrons.

woman, Ursula Cotta. She belonged to one of the noblest, most pious families of Eisenach, and in her house Luther was introduced to a large circle of distinguished people. What he learned in this home stayed with him for life. The happy hours in Frau Ursula Cotta's house explain why he always remembered Eisenach with gratitude.

He was now ready for the university. Instead of sending him to the easily accessible neighborhood university at Leipzig, the father chose the municipal university at Erfurt. It may have been for the reason that Erfurt enjoyed a greater reputation for scholarship.

A great deal is known about the organization of medieval universities, and Luther's first year as a student conformed to the established routine. Living conditions as well as academic studies were minutely regulated, and nothing unusual can be reported about the student Luther. In later years he complained bitterly about the formalistic character of the instruction; yet he would have been unable to hold his own in his long conflict with the medieval scholastics if he had not been so thoroughly conversant with their methods. He freely admitted that the prescribed exercises in argumentation sharpened his natural aptitude for dialectics. Even as a student he excelled as a debater, so that he acquired the nickname "the philosopher."

It is significant that Luther formed no contact with the circle of humanists at Erfurt. They did not become important until after Luther had already entered the monastery. But he did familiarize himself with the "modern" theology of Occam whose thesis that reason by itself is incapable of understanding the truths of revelation made an indelible impression on Luther. Later on he was able to restate this theology with great power and originality. The broad-minded Occamist theologians introduced Luther to the then "modern" theories about the cosmos; in this manner he also acquired a very solid but independent knowledge of the Aristotelian system. When Luther in February, 1505 received his master's degree with customary academic formality, nothing had yet shaken his faith and no unusual religious experience had yet occurred to him.

As the young academic dignitary entered upon the study of law, he went through the first of a series of events which gradually forced his life into a new direction. We sense something of his first conversion. On July 2, 1505, he returned from a vacation which, for some unknown reason, he had taken in the middle of the semester. While he was still several miles away from Erfurt a heavy thunderstorm overtook him at Schlotterheim and a bolt of lightning struck the ground close to him. The pressure threw him several yards and he exclaimed in panic, "Help, St. Anna, I want to become a monk."

Though we cannot know accurately what led to this sudden decision, we may assume that it came as the climax of a long inward struggle. After he had completed his work for the master's degree and before he began his studies at the faculty of law, he had enjoyed a period of leisure. During that period he had meditated about matters of faith in a manner quite characteristic of him. He himself revealed later that he had been gravely troubled by the *tentatio tristitiae,* that is, dread concerning his sins. It was the tenderness of his conscience which prompted him to adhere to his vow, though he received much advice to the contrary. By July 16 his affairs had been put in order and he could invite his friends to a final get-together. The following morning his friends accompanied him to the gates of the Black Monastery of the Augustinian friars. "Today you can still see me, but never again," were his parting words to the friends as the gates closed behind him. He was very serious in his resolve. That is all we know. This earnestness led to some of the most severe mental agonies of his life.

One can see a striking parallel in the life of St. Augustine. The church father also awakened to the earnestness of life as he read the pseudo-Ciceronian essay of Hortensius, but reached the full assurance of faith only much later in the garden at Milan. Luther's entry into the monastery was only the first step in the new direction. The full implications appeared much later after a long and painful struggle.

Birth of the Reformation

The Reformation opened a new era. In one way or another that fact is generally admitted. It is, then, a purely spiritual event which calls the modern age into being. It became a reality in one of those extremely rare moments when an individual comes face to face with God.

But the average Protestant, as far as he knows anything about it, is inclined to view it in a different light. For him the Reformation makes its appearance by a show of strength. It began on October 31, 1517, when Martin Luther nailed his ninety-five theses to the doors of the Castle Church in Wittenberg. For our purpose it is immaterial when it became a custom to observe this day as the Festival of the Reformation. The first really enthusiastic celebration occurred in connection with the tercentenary in 1817. The young romantic movement, which revered the past, responded with intense feeling to the anniversary of Luther's deed. We know of this observance and how the age looked upon Luther from illustrations and proclamations that have been preserved. He was "the hero of the faith," the man who had successfullly "broken the chains of the Middle Ages." [1] Progress became

---

[1] Thus began the misleading identification of the Reformation and so-called progress. The celebration at Leipzig attempted to symbolize this "progress." A parade was held in which the three faiths participated. A rabbi was in the lead, followed by a Roman Catholic priest, and the Lutheran clergy of the city came last. This notion of progress appealed to the generation which was passing from the age of the Enlightenment to the era of romanticism.

a carefully cultivated and popular idea in the nineteenth century. It was the great age of interest in history, when men liked to think in terms of "epochal changes" and "heroes." The average reader enjoyed the dramatic element in history and found the essence of the Reformation in this "act of faith."

It is no coincidence that sober historical research has recently corrected this notion of the Reformation. It had its origin, after all, in the indifference of the nineteenth century, whose already secularized faith could no longer understand the depth of Luther's religious experience. The real beginnings of the Reformation are actually less spectacular and more radical. We must seek them in the innermost recesses of a man's soul. He was not interested in a heroic pose that would impress the world. In dread and deep loneliness he encountered God, and the solemnity of that moment was far greater than the appearance before the emperor and the princes of the realm. Luther returned to Wittenberg in 1511. His order, particularly his superior Johannes von Staupitz, expected great things of young brother Martin whose outstanding ability must have been evident from the start. This provost of the Augustinian order, a nobleman by blood and temperament, was a gifted administrator and kind shepherd of souls, for whom Luther retained a life-long feeling of gratitude and affection.

In 1508 Luther had been assigned to a temporary instructorship at the University of Wittenberg, but he was soon recalled to Erfurt by the superiors of his order. He was sent back to Wittenberg in 1511, this time with the rank of full professor as successor to Johannes von Staupitz. His departure from Erfurt apparently involved some unpleasantness. It seems that his rapid rise in the order caused envy among some brothers and even superiors.

Who could have foreseen at the time that Luther was to spend the remainder of his life in the drab little community of less than two thousand inhabitants? Luther himself would have been the last to predict that this town "at the very edge of civilization," as he called it, would ever become the center of world shaking events.

At that time he suffered severe inner conflicts. We know that during his stay at the monastery he had eagerly engaged in all the pious practices which the medieval church recommended for the salvation of souls. Luther still looked upon the monastery as a refuge which could guarantee eternal salvation. But he could find no assurance in the countless spiritual exercises, the many opportunities for self-examination, and the pronouncements of ecclesiastical absolution. He obtained no relief. In the kind of spiritual crisis he experienced, the number of observances makes little difference because the crisis itself stems from the search for a new kind of life. The most minute examination of the state of his conscience still left him dissatisfied. Whatever aids to the religious life were available in the monastery, Bible reading and breviary, theological and other studies, were pressed into service with the same penetrating earnestness, and directed towards his great inner need. Here was no trail blazer of a new civilization or hero, a role in which a liberal age liked to cast him afterward. He did contend for the faith and the spirit but he did so as a man who suffered intensely. While it is not immediately apparent, he actually anticipated the religious struggles of the following centuries and fought them through in his own soul. Even in Nietzsche's pathetic agonies we can still find traces of Luther's own struggle with God. Personal suffering enabled Luther to describe a state of mind which few other Christian teachers have known as intimately as he—anguish.

But what was it? Not an overt difficulty, like the rule of chastity which the monastic order imposed upon its members. Luther had little trouble in that respect. It was not an intellectual conflict between the newly emerging philosophy and the traditional biblical view of the universe. Such interpretations are projections of a modern mind and have nothing to do with the real need of Luther. His anxiety goes deeper. It involved his total existence. He had to know whether he could stand before God at all. He felt that he was lost unless he could find an answer to this question.

Modern man no longer asks this question and must therefore credit Luther with some other achievement. The ideas of freedom of conscience (whatever that may mean), of release from ecclesiastical controls, and other readily grasped slogans, have deprived him of the ability to understand what is involved: a human being pleading with God for his very existence.

Luther's whole quest appears obscure to modern man because it moves in another direction and is couched in the language and thought forms of the late Middle Ages. It should cause no great surprise that Luther thought in terms which his monastic education had made familiar to him. But the difference between Luther and us goes deeper than the use of words. It goes back to the fact that for us the question about "existence itself" has almost disappeared. It is not altogether extinct. One still confronts it in some of the great literary characters which Knut Hamsun, Dostoevski, Dwinger, Juenger, André Gide, and other modern authors have created. Its strongest manifestation is still the life work of Nietzsche and his revolt against God. These men were all worlds apart from Luther, but all of them knew something of the one question and the one decision on which man's total existence might suffer shipwreck. This basic question presented itself to Luther in the dilemma "the justice of God."

In the dark night of his despair he had at times noticed a consoling light. Staupitz had helped him with a few unforgettable words. He was the first to tell Luther that anguish is part of a normal Christian experience; he had admonished him to overcome his scrupulosity, this arch-enemy of genuine repentance. He had reminded him of the difference between real and imaginary sins and, best of all, directed him to the person of Christ as a source of genuine comfort. How much theological and pastoral wisdom is reflected in his advice to the tortured young monk: God is not angry with you, you are angry with God.

Luther himself has related the circumstances under which he found his answer. It is still a moving experience to read the description of that decisive hour in the preface to the Latin edition of his *Works* which the aging Reformer had prepared a year before he died. There is a happiness in these lines which is not of this earth. They belong to the classic documents in which great Christians have described how the encounter with God affected their souls. Luther's testimony ranks with Augustine's recital of his garden experience and Pascal's famous memorial of 1654.

Luther writes: "I hated the term 'Justice of God,' for I had been taught by the practice and disputations of the doctors to understand it philosophically as a formal or active justice by which God himself is righteous and punishes the sinner and unjust. I could not love the righteous God who punishes the sinner and I hated him. Though I had lived as a virtuous monk, I felt myself as a sinner before God and was restless in my conscience and dared not hope that I could become reconciled by my own efforts. I was displeased with God and said: Is it not enough that I, a miserable sinner, through the fall have been condemned in all eternity and burdened by the ten commandments and other evil? Must God in his gospel add greater agony and threaten me through the gospel with his wrath and justice? Thus I angrily rushed around in my bewildered conscience but I hit violently upon this statement by St. Paul,[1] driven by a consuming thirst to find out what St. Paul meant. Then God had compassion on me. I meditated day and night until I noticed the connection of the words: 'For therein is the righteousness of God revealed as it is written: The just shall live by faith.' Then I began to understand the righteousness of God as the kind of righteousness which enables the just to live by the gift of God, i.e. 'by faith.' The gospel makes the justice of God manifest, that is, the so-called passive justice by which God justifies us by faith out of his mercy and compassion, as it is written: The just shall live by faith.

"I felt like one who had been born again. The doors had swung open and I had entered into paradise itself. At once the Scriptures presented a different face to me. I examined the passages I could remember and discovered the same meaning in others. For instance: the 'work of God' means the work God does; the 'power of God' means the power by which God strengthens us. The 'wisdom of God' is the wisdom by which he makes us wise. As I had hated the words 'righteousness of God' with a deep hatred, I now favored the same words with ardent love as something sweet and lovable. This passage of Paul became my *porta paradisi,* a real gateway to paradise."

Luther's work room was located in the tower of the Black Monastery at Wittenberg and the new insight came to him in the quiet of his own study. The event is therefore usually

---

[1] The gospel . . . is the power of God unto salvation . . . For therein is the righteousness of God revealed from faith to faith: as it is written, The just shall live by faith (Rom. 1:16f.).

described as "the tower experience." Because this new understanding of the Scriptures soon found its way into Luther's lectures on exegesis at the university, we can date it with considerable accuracy. It happened during the winter semester 1512-13, probably in the spring of 1513.

In this hour the Reformation was born. Without it, the world would have never seen the ninety-five theses or the Diet at Worms. A new epoch in history began because of one man's struggle for God.

There is a difference between Luther's experience and that of the modern seeker after God; the difference is decisive in spite of certain superficial similarities. Modern man encounters God as a self-directed ego in the pride of his selfhood and is necessarily broken in the encounter because he is unable to yield his autonomy. Luther surrendered wholly to God and in this act found not only God the judge but God the giver, not only the God of wrath but the God of grace. Thus he discovered the pathway from despair into a new life.

Beautiful, like a spiritual springtime, are Luther's teachings during those first quiet years after the agony had come to an end. His fame did not yet stand between him and his hearers. What had been given to him was forcefully and ably presented in his lectures and exercises. Though a new period in history had dawned, nothing happened for a few years except a gradual change in the orientation of a theologian. It came about because a Christian man had found a solution for his human anxiety in the liberating truth of God's grace through Christ. Some of his finest literary works were composed at this time and precede the famous theses by some months. Though they are formally directed against scholastic theology, they are actually statements of the great truth which Luther had found: solace comes to men through the grace of God. The new content of his theology even affects Luther's methods. The same tender yet forceful sentiments are expressed in some of his early letters.

Even after the courageous deed of October 31, 1517, had made him overnight the most famous man in Germany and moved him into the very center of public affairs, the glow of these early years still lingers over a document of utmost theological importance, the theses for the disputation at Heidelberg in 1518. Here particularly, but not exclusively, appears the veritable revolution in theology which came as a result of Luther's fundamentally new position. The glorified human ego breaks down because God is not at man's disposal, either in pious practices or in the events of history, either in the life of the individual or in the life of the church. As man accepts this limitation, as he no longer craves to rule but is ready to receive, he discovers the very spot where God is actually accessible to man: in Christ the crucified. These are reflections which are valid for all times, and Luther appears almost modern when he insists on man's utter incapacity to discover God either in nature or history. At least, man cannot do it by himself. Nature and history, as the philosopher Hamann pointed out much later, "remain silent for the skeptic." God must reveal himself, if man is to find him. He does it because he is a giving God. "In Jesus Christ is all true theology and knowledge of God." As we contemplate him, we learn that God does not wish to withhold knowledge of himself from us. But our standard of values is changed in the process. The outstanding, recognized, prominent people and institutions are really not important in the world. Rather the will of God is realized through suffering and the cross and through small, insignificant things. We cannot even indicate here how important this new viewpoint became for the spiritual history of the West. The Reformation itself proves the importance of this hidden law of God in the course of events.

Hand in hand with the change in Luther's personal affairs, there occurred a change in the affairs of Europe which reveals to us God's work in and through history. Wittenberg, which acquired not only European but world-wide fame through Luther, was actually at the edge of civilization. It was not a part of the old territory to which German cultural life had been confined. The *limes,* the ancient fortified wall of the Romans, was also the boundary line of German civilization. A rich cultural life had grown up behind the protection of this wall. It derived its inspiration from the Greco-Roman civilization and had flourished here since the days of the Roman Empire. Colonization and missionary activities had added new lands in time, but they remained without a tradition. It was precisely in the territories that had enjoyed a rich cultural heritage for many centuries that the Reformation met the most subborn resistance. The supporters of the Reformation, and thereby the harbingers of a new era, were the young universities. They were located in the provinces which had never felt the weight of the ancient tradition, and new ideas had a chance to take root here and become historically effective. It was not only the fact that people here were more impartial. It was again that hidden law in history to which Luther referred in the Heidelberg disputation (I Cor. 1:27-29). St. Paul had already recognized it as God's way with the world. It had been operative from the days of the prophets to our own. God has chosen that which is unpretentious in the world and chosen it as the place for the demonstration of his majesty. It is the law of the lowliness of Christ and it applies equally to his church.

That the quiet hour in the tower of the Black Monastery was actually the birth hour of a new epoch and that the law of God's hidden direction becomes particularly manifest here, can readily be seen if we compare the inner experience with the public announcement of it.

The actual publication of the theses was anything but a bid for publicity. No crowd, either students or citizens, surrounded the "Reformer" and nobody thought it a momentous occasion for the simple reason that there were no onlookers. Luther and his *famulus* Agricola were alone.

The traffic in indulgences which perverted genuine remorse, as Luther himself had known it, from a deeply religious experience into a commercial transaction, had long been offensive. Many others besides Luther had objected to it. Luther, who served not only as a professor but also as pastor of the Wittenberg parish church, had learned at firsthand how corruptive the practice was. His experiences as confessor convinced him that something had to be done. When he urged his parishioners to show true repentance, it occurred with increasing frequency that they produced their indulgence papers which promised release from the pains of hell and particularly from purgatory. It is characteristic of Luther that at first he did not contemplate anything resembling a public protest but planned instead for an academic debate. By a scholarly discussion he wished to clarify the thinking of the church on the subject of "the power of indulgences." Indulgences had not yet been defined as part of the Catholic dogma. Every teacher of theology was therefore entitled to make them the subject of debate. For that reason Luther had prepared a number of theses and, in approved academic fashion, invited discussion. Because they were only intended for the perusal of theologians he had written them in Latin and affixed them to the doors of the Castle Church which served as a sort of bulletin board. Luther did not wish to exclude the public, but the public to which he appealed were the scholars, and he proceeded in every detail according to official ecclesiastical regulations. Because he was not unaware of the possible consequences of his action, he had prepared himself by earnest prayer.

Yet no one except his student assistant, Johann Schneider of Eisleben, who after the custom of the times had taken the Latin name Agricola, accompanied him at that fateful noon hour of October 31, 1517. It was the day before All Souls, a holy day on which the Elector used to display his famous collection of relics for the inspection of the people.

Those were the circumstances under which the theses were made public. Nobody accepted Luther's challenge to a debate. For two weeks there was no reaction of any kind. But that was only the lapse of time which the spark needed to erupt in an explosion. The tempest broke. After some hesitation Luther had sent copies of the theses to a few friends. Without his approval, and probably against his wishes, they were placed in circulation and, with a speed entirely unprecedented at the time, they went all over Germany. Albrecht Dürer expressed his approval of the monk, who was personally unknown to him, by presenting him with some woodcuts and copper engravings. The storm which raged through Germany was so violent that Luther felt as though his breath had been taken away. It seemed to him that he had attempted nothing less than to "storm the heavens and set the world on fire." As the reactions increased and the repercussions widened, Luther recognized that a conflict of worldwide dimensions was in the making.

"The melody became too high for my voice." The deep concern he had felt as a theologian and pastor had prompted his lone action; what he had done was based upon his new understanding of the Scriptures. But Luther had never anticipated or intended that his action of October 31 would mark a conclusive turning point in history.

In order to appreciate the significance of that event we must take two factors into consideration. Luther's personal conduct in all this turmoil was a continuation of the course on which he had started in faith and obedience. He simply could not reconcile the sale of indulgences, either in theory or practice, with the new understanding of God's grace and forgiveness that had come to him in his tower experience.

With extraordinary perspicacity he developed his thelogical attack upon this abuse, but he did it in such a manner that it aimed at the heart of the religious practices and even the soteriology of the medieval church. When the theses received an overwhelming reception, Luther's action became politically and historically so important that it distinguished his undertaking from all previous attempts at a reformation. It is really true: a movement of world-changing power had begun as the religious experience of one man.

Luther had no desire to become a figure in history. None of his "deeds" were ever prompted by a craving for power; in fact he had a lifelong disdain for it. One might judge superficially that as a "genius" he had no need for the display of power but actually Luther was oblivious of it because he was content to let God direct his way. Only as he remained obedient to the truth which God had revealed to him could his life work become an effective force in history. Nothing can change this fact: the new era came in as result of the spiritual experience of one lone individual.

What about the papacy? It is almost unbelievable how lightly Rome treated this first phase of a great historical upheaval. After Luther had dutifully informed his bishop, Hieronymus Schulze, of his step, this kindhearted but very insignificant dignitary expressed his approval in a casual but generally friendly letter. The very busy and very money-minded Archbishop Albrecht of Mainz whom Luther had notified at the same time, turned the matter over to his advisers, who, in time-honored bureaucratic fashion, deposited the memorandum on somebody's desk. The indifference of these immediate superiors may not mean too much, but it is amazing to see how long it took the curia to recognize the import of these events. Not until Cardinal Cajetan arrived in Augsburg in 1519 was a serious attempt made to clarify the theological issues which were involved in this conflict. One cannot help but conclude that this blindness shows how fully the Church of Rome deserved the judgment of history, in the course of which half of her followers were to turn away from her.

Worms

Carlyle, in his admiration for the heroic element in history, was frequently inclined to confuse the great and the merely dramatic. As Hilaire Belloc, one of his most brilliant critics, has pointed out, he often preferred eloquence to the simple facts of a situation. But Carlyle's characterization of the Diet of Worms is accurate. It was the most decisive and most important event in modern history.

The true church of God moves quietly through this world. That which fills the atmosphere with splendor and fanfare has usually little meaning for the Kingdom of God on earth. What rulers such as Napoleon and Frederick the Great contributed to the life of the church is negligible, and the church has carried on under other great political leaders as though they had not existed at all. By the same token, great events have often taken place in the life of the church which were not recognized by the world. That has always been so, from the time when Christ and his apostles worked unnoticed under the eyes of Caesars and emperors until our own day.

The Diet of Worms is in every respect an exception. World history and Kingdom history are joined here. It is one of those rare moments in history when secular and church history merge into one. It occurred on April 17, 18, 1521, and we rightfully look upon these days as moments of a great transition.

How did these days impress an observer? Anyone who

was in the city of Worms on these days must have known that something important was in the air. The town which had a normal population of seven thousand inhabitants was crowded with visitors. The young emperor was there and attracted the curious but well-meaning attention of everyone. The princes of the realm had turned out in unusual numbers. The papal *nuntius* Alexander, one of the few men who realized the importance of the event, excitedly sent one dispatch after another to Rome. His reports give us a very detailed, though not always accurate, account of the proceedings.

Though the most illustrious dignitaries of the time were assembled at Worms, the one man on whom all attention was centered was Martin Luther. As far as the limited means of communication made it possible, people had followed the triumphant journey which took the monk of Wittenberg through the heart of Germany. It was public knowledge that the diplomats had long debated whether Luther should be permitted to appear at all before the emperor and the princes. Only few people realized that it was Luther's own Elector who had insisted upon Luther's personal appearance, until the others were finally willing to make that concession. Up to the last minute the papists had done everything in their power to prevent the presence of the Augustinian monk. There had been unmistakable threats. People remembered the fate of the unfortunate John Huss who, notwithstanding an imperial guarantee of personal safety, was burned at the stake during the Diet of Constance. When Luther decided to ignore all dangers, and started confidently on his journey, a great popular demonstration was the answer to this display of faith and courage. A statement of Luther was repeated everywhere: "If they should start a bonfire between Wittenberg and Worms that would reach up to heaven because they had so much time to stir it, I would still go in God's name and step right into the mouth of Behemoth, stand between his big teeth, confess Christ and surrender myself to him." It became known that he had turned down a last warning by the Elector's own confessor. "If there were as many devils in Worms as there are shingles on the roofs, I shall go there."

The journey turned into a triumph. The faculty and students of his alma mater, the University of Erfurt, led by the rector, received him at the outskirts of the city and honored him like a prince. On Sunday, *Misericordias Domini,* he preached before a large congregation in the church of his order on the Gospel for the Day. An eyewitness records that the church was so crowded "that the gallery began to crack and every one was afraid that it would collapse. Some therefore began to break windows and would have jumped into the cemetery had Luther not quieted them and told them to stand still. The devil was making an apparition, no harm would befall them—and nothing happened." Luther's sermon of that day has been preserved and shows how Luther felt as he approached Worms. The whole sermon treats of the gospel of God's saving grace and only one passing remark alludes to the reason for this momentous journey. "I know very well that they do not like to hear it. Just the same, I shall tell the truth and must do it, if it should cost me twenty necks, so that judgment should not come upon me."

On the morning of April 16, several noblemen on horseback had gone out in the early morning hours to meet him. When a trumpet signal from the cathedral tower announced his arrival, a customary greeting for distinguished visitors, the constables had their hands full to restrain the crowd. At ten o'clock in the morning Luther made his triumphant entry into the city. The small carriage in which he and three companions had made the long journey was preceded by Imperial Herald Kaspar Sturm, who carried the imperial writ of safe conduct. A milling crowd, which by now had swelled to several thousand spectators, forced the procession to travel slowly through the city streets.

This popular sentiment, a mixture of curiosity, enthusiasm, and sensationalism, merits a critical evaluation. Were all these people who lined the streets Christians in the grip of a newly awakened spiritual fervor? Such an assertion would be naive. For countless people Luther had become a national symbol; national feelings, though vague, were always present under the surface. A few years earlier, Erasmus on his journey along the Rhine had become the recipient of a similar demonstration and was mildly surprised by it. For he, better than his easily aroused German admirers, knew that he had no claim to such an ovation. But in Luther the national consciousness found its first worthy object, and that seems to support the contention of those who see in the Reformation primarily a phenomenon of German nationalism. It is quite true that there had never been a day when German national feeling arose as spontaneously as it did at Worms, but the essential aspect of this intense emotion dare not be ignored. It was directed towards the concerns of the faith. A religious decision was reached here, of great significance not only for the nation but for the future of Europe itself.

Luther appeared before two sessions of the Diet. April 17, during the late afternoon hours, he was first ushered into the chambers of the episcopal residence. Ulrich von Pappenheim and Imperial Herald Kaspar Sturm called for him around four o'clock in the afternoon and, in order to avoid the mob, led him by a circuitous route into the episcopal palace where the Diet was assembled. But his case was not heard until six o'clock, and then came the moment itself when he stood literally before the emperor and the princes of the realm. It was only a brief and formal arraignment, devoid in itself of any real historic significance. From contemporary portraits we can form a very clear picture of the two leading personalities. The young emperor had already decided that it was to be his life work "to risk all his dominions, his friends, body and blood, life and soul for the preservation of the Catholic faith and Catholic Church." For that reason he could see nothing in Luther but an obstinate heretic, whose motives he understood as little as his language. At this youthful age the emperor appeared even more pale than later in life and the characteristic Habsburg chin protruded more markedly than later, when he carried himself with unmistakable imperial dignity.

A copper engraving by Lucas Cranach gives a likeness of Luther in 1521—a powerful profile, a firm forehead, highly arched brows, and mouth and chin which expressed strong determination. But no artist has ever been able to reproduce the most characteristic feature of this face—the sparkle of his dark eyes which impressed some observers as demoniacal and others as brilliant. A contemporary said of them that "they glittered and gleamed like a star so that no one could really look into them."

The foreign diplomats who, like many of the German princes, saw the famous monk for the first time and had expected a sensation, were disappointed. The deputy of the archbishop of Trier, Dr. Johannes von der Ecken, had been instructed to ask two questions of Luther. Was he the author of the books in front of him, and was he willing to repudiate them in part or in whole? After looking at the titles, Luther affirmed the first question but asked for time to consider the second, a request which could not readily be denied. He was told that he must have his answer ready the following day, and that he would have to speak freely without the use of a manuscript. That ended the session. Luther was immediately

returned to his quarters. Because he spoke very softly, probably on the advice of his Elector in order not to appear bold,
the impression got around that he was frightened. His opponents, who "had been struck as if by thunder" by his courageous appearance, were now convinced that this whole matter
would be settled easily and quickly.

On the following day the meeting was moved to the
largest assembly room in the episcopal palace, but so many
people had crowded in that even the princes were compelled
to stand. It was again six o'clock and so dark that torches
had to be lighted. Once more Dr. von der Ecken opened the
proceedings and Luther gave a full answer to the question
whether he would be willing to repudiate his books. His
address was brief and clear, he gave it in a strong voice and
in German. The speech probably lasted less than ten minutes.
Upon request, he repeated it immediately in Latin. He acknowledged his writings which could be divided into three
classes: devotional books, books against the papacy, and po-
lemical writings against individuals. No one was interested
in the disavowal of the first group. He could not retract any
of his writings against the tyranny of the papacy which
weighed so heavily even upon the "highly renowned German
nation." The same answer applied to the third group. He
asked that anyone who could correct him from the Scriptures,
wherever he was in error, should by the grace of God do so.
Only in this manner could he see any solution of the discord
for which he was held responsible. It could not be settled by
condemning the Word of God. That would be an ill beginning for the reign of the young emperor in whom everyone
placed such high hopes.

Because Luther's reply had not been a curt refusal but a
polite answer in which he expressed his willingness to be
convinced by sound biblical reasons, the princes, who met

immediately afterward, found themselves in a difficult situation. They could not simply ignore such an offer, but they could even less admit a disputation over matters of faith which had already been decided by the church. The emperor was particularly opposed to such a course. As a compromise it was finally decided to inquire once more of Luther whether he was willing to recant. When Dr. von der Ecken in a full session of the diet asked that question, Luther gave that memorable answer which made him and the diet famous. "Since Your Majesty and Your Graces demand a plain answer, I shall give one without horns or teeth. Unless I am convinced by the testimony of the Scriptures or clear reason—I cannot believe in either popes or councils alone, for it is evident that they have frequently erred and contradicted themselves—I am overcome in my conscience by the passages of Scriptures I have quoted and I am caught in the Word of God. I therefore cannot and will not retract, for it is neither safe nor salutary to do anything against the conscience."

Obviously aware of the tremendous import of his refusal, he added in the same clear voice in German, the ejaculation of the mercenaries which he often used as a closing prayer in his sermons, "God help me. Amen."

After a brief exchange of comments between the emperor and Dr. Ecken, the former nodded and Luther was escorted from the room. At this moment a tumult arose, because several German noblemen thought that Luther had been arrested and was to be taken to prison. When Luther reassured them by gestures, they followed him, gaily raising their arms and spreading their fingers in the manner of victorious lancers. Luther did likewise when he returned to his inn, the *Johanniterhof,* and exclaimed happily, "I am through it, I am through it!"

That was the day at Worms as posterity remembers it. It

is too often forgotten that the next few days were far more difficult than the trial itself. There began behind the scenes a series of private conferences and negotiations in order to reach some understanding with Luther. Several of the negotiators who undertook this task were men of great scholarship and personal integrity. It was not easy for Luther, who was alone during these meetings as he had been during the trial. He was not subjected to threats or demands but to persuasion. Much was made of the need for unity, a subject that is always close to the heart of all politicians.

Yet, the two leading protagonists remained firm, Luther and the emperor. The final break, which had appeared inevitable for some time, finally came on April 25. On that day, Dr. Eck appeared with the imperial secretary, Siebenbürger, at Luther's inn and informed him in Latin that in view of the futility of all admonitions, the emperor as the secular head of the church was compelled to take action against him. His safe conduct was valid for another three weeks. He must immediately cease preaching, teaching, and writing. Luther withdrew for a few minutes of silent prayer and upon his return expressed his gratitude to the emperor and the princes for the hearing they had granted him. He stated his readiness to suffer death and disgrace for the emperor and the realm, but he must reserve for himself the free proclamation of the Word of God.

The next morning, April 26, two carriages left by the Martin's gate and their departure caused little attention. On the open highway a detachment of mounted Saxon mercenaries "waylaid" him and took him to the Wartburg where he was safe from the reach of hostile forces and could find leisure for one of the most valuable accomplishments of his life, the translation of the New Testament.

Augsburg

One issue, which occupied every diet during the first few decades of the Reformation has become almost unintelligible to the modern reader. It was concerned with the legal status of Protestantism. It appears so strange to us, because in the intervening centuries a new idea has become firmly fixed in the modern mind: religion is the private affair of each individual. That a man's beliefs ultimately concern no one but him alone is a fundamentally new idea from which both good and evil results have sprung. There are some distinct advantages. Ever since there have been two churches in the West, that element of personal decision, which is for us an essential ingredient of every genuine religious conviction, has also been there. Ranke was the first to notice it. As long as there was only one unified Christian church, men grew into it as a matter of course. When that unity ceased, membership in the Christian church was only possible through membership in one particular branch of it, and called thereby for personal choice. In that respect the Reformation tended towards a personal commitment and furthered the religious life.

But the transition to a religious faith which was a purely personal matter entailed also a danger. As time went on, religion retreated from public life until the nineteenth century was satisfied with the weakest possible formula: religion is the private affair of the individual. The Socialist movement adroitly adopted this slogan and insisted that the party as such had no interest in the religious beliefs of its members. The extremists soon dropped this bourgeois point of view and substituted a regime where religion was no longer the concern of the individual. Religion itself became "socialized." In other words, it became subject to dictation from above. Yet the notion of the purely private character of religion is so much a part of modern life itself that it becomes very difficult for us to understand the basically different approach of the Reformation to this subject. In the eyes of the Reformers the Christian church and the Christian faith are not sole concerns of the individual. In this respect the Reformers retained the medieval outlook. If internal or external changes occurred in the status of the church, they called for legislative action. The possibility of ignoring the schism or of relegating the religious issue to the conscience of the individual was unthinkable for an emperor like Charles V, who looked upon himself as the secular head of the Christian world and defender of the Church of Rome. This was a public issue and everyone was agreed that it could only be settled on a nation-wide basis. The religious question was thus thrown into the diet, the representative of the body politic. The decade from 1521-30 was the classical period during which Protestantism created its political structure. The process began at Worms and came to a temporary halt at Augsburg. Two very interesting diets had met in the meantime. In a communication to the Diet at Nuremberg in 1523, Pope Hadrian had acknowledged the guilt of the Roman Church. Had his spiritual leadership and understanding prevailed, the Christian world might yet live in the unity of one faith and one church.

It was at the Diet of Speyer in 1529 that the Evangelicals were first referred to as "Protestants." But before Protestantism was in a position to build its own political structure, it had to go through the bitter strife and fateful consequences of the Peasants' War. The unrest among the peasants, the lowest stratum in medieval society, was ultimately caused by social pressures. The Reformation did not create these pressures but it did provide the occasion for their violent eruption. We find, therefore, that social reformers and budding revolutionaries first presented their demands in biblical language and supported them with biblical arguments. That can be partly explained by the linguistic habits of the time. It is also evidence of the inspiration which the religious renewal had furnished and which had now begun to affect the political order. At first Luther, quite naturally, sided with the peasants. It is amazing how quickly he reversed himself. Within the span of a few weeks, initial approval had turned into bitter condemnation; so harshly did Luther write against the peasants that his essay has often been characterized as sheer cruelty. Very few other books by the Reformer have been as severely criticized, and it is claimed that his popularity waned from that time on and that the decline was justified.

What were the facts? The peasant uprising had reached its peak in May, 1525. Brutally pillaging, the peasants rushed through the countryside like a gigantic red flood. It became instantly clear that a social order becomes demoniacal if it falls into the hands of "enthusiasts"—fanatics who wish to remake church and public life in accordance with their principle of "pure spirit." Not only the political structure but all social and community life was threatened with collapse and chaos. One need only take the measure of Thomas Münzer, Luther's antagonist in this conflict, in order to ascertain the difference between the two men and the true greatness of the Reformer. Only prejudice can insist that Münzer was the true and consistent representative of a new order. We still need an objective biography of this brilliant but confused man. In the last analysis he was nothing more than a mixture of demagogue and dilettante, just as all demagogues are ultimately dilettantes. They are rarely equal to life's realities. No one can say that the future of Europe would have been safe in the hands of Münzer and his followers. Even to be a fair-minded spokesman for the oppressed required more than he could give.

Luther's position is, therefore, not unreasonable. Revolutionary anarchy offered no solution. Luther could not but take a stand against the rebels, as much in the interest of public welfare as for the sake of his own life work.

The question remains whether one can justify the extreme violence of his pronouncements. They cannot be excused merely on the basis that he made them at a moment when the situation was extremely critical. No decision of policy had yet been made when he wrote, and the reluctance of Elector Frederick to act in the face of the approaching mobs struck terror into every heart. Luther's position must be understood in the light of two other facts. The advance of the rebels was marked by utmost cruelty. No reference to the Scriptures could justify looting and violence. On the contrary, it was intolerable that men should cover up such conduct by quotations from the Bible. It would have been strange indeed if Luther had not protested against it. Luther was also distressed by the failure of the rulers who were doubly guilty. At first they had contributed to the evil by their lack of social consciousness, and now, in the hour of grave danger, they were hesitant, even frightened. "He that ruleth, must rule with diligence." He who is entrusted with the preservation of law and order must discharge this trust. A prince who has a responsibility before God must exercise this responsibility, even if he has to take up the sword. He dare not be cowardly about it. Luther's terrible advice that one should exterminate the peasants like mad dogs loses its fierceness the moment one realizes that it applied to frenzied rebels who raged like rabid dogs. In dealing with such animals one can act on only one principle: unless I can destroy you, you will destroy me. One may disagree with Luther's diagnosis of the situation; if it was the correct one, however, there was no alternative.

It is a foolish and unwarranted conclusion that this incident establishes Luther as a "tool of the princes." The man who stood before them at Worms, who fearlessly confronted Duke George of Saxony, who frequently and in sometimes stern, even rude, language reminded rulers of their duties, who publicly proclaimed that God would punish them all in his wrath—this man was no timeserver. The often quoted formula "throne and altar" has nothing to do with Luther, in fact it distorts his position.

Later on Luther had no choice but to place the political fate of the Reformation into the hands of the princes, for there was no one else who could accept this trust. To expect any other development is to demand that Luther, in addition to everything else, should have changed the whole juridical structure of the empire. Yet in 1525 all these issues had not come into question.

A famous historian of the nineteenth century, after a careful analysis of the facts, has expressed the opinion that the year 1525 represents the zenith in Luther's life. That appraisal is correct.

Had he decided upon any other course, his whole life work would have been drawn into the whirlpool of conflicting political currents. With intuitive insight he found his way through the confusions and complications of the moment. He could only continue in the manner in which he had begun. Not expediency but obedience towards the divine order was to determine his position. It was a great moment in his life when he made his decision, regardless of its effect upon his popularity. With one stroke he risked the good will and support of the masses. It is perhaps the surest proof of his greatness that he had the strength to take this stand. Who would venture to say that our generation has nothing to learn from Luther in that respect?

It is frequently claimed that Luther should never have allowed his popularity to wane. Such an assertion is sheer superficiality. Fairness should recognize that in this extremely critical situation Luther could not permit any ulterior motive to influence his judgment.

The continued growth of Protestantism as a corporate body is another proof of the wholesomeness of Luther's position.

That the common people did not look upon Protestantism as the party of wealth and privilege is shown abundantly by the fact that they were often the ones who, frequently in dramatic showdowns, compelled their magistrates to introduce the Reformation in their cities.

It remains a fact that neither the support of the gentry nor the equally obnoxious idol "public opinion" was given an opportunity to influence the course of the Reformation.

The flux of political fortunes ended in a temporary stalemate. The emperor had been firmly determined to take action against the Protestants, but the exigencies of the political situation forced him to one postponement after another. The foreign policy of the emperor, by no means always in the interest of Germany, frequently offered the Evangelicals a respite. Luther was confirmed in his faith that even the great leaders of men are only puppets whom God has placed on the stage of history and manipulates for his purposes. God had indeed directed the course of events in such a manner that, after the first decade, Protestantism could no longer be treated as a mere heresy that could be stamped out at will.

The divine background of all historical processes is as recognizable in the Reformation as it is in the events of secular history. That was the situation in 1530 when a diet was summoned to Augsburg to clarify the issues.

Though this diet was of far-reaching importance for the Reformation, Luther was unable to attend in person. Deprived of a chance to stand in the front ranks in this battle, he had to entrust the defense and protection of his work to others. It was a severe test for Luther, but an announcement to the world that this movement was no longer Luther's own. It had now become the concern of Christendom.

Luther had to stay away because he was under the imperial ban, and even the courageous magistrates of Augsburg refused him hospitality while the diet was in session.[1]

The details of this meeting, therefore, belong only partly in a biography of Luther. The Reformer himself was compelled to follow the proceedings from his quarters at the distant fortress of Coburg. He was kept informed, but too slowly and irregularly, he thought, to satisfy his restless mind. In his deep concern, he felt that he should have been consulted more frequently and more quickly. Divine providence, however, had chosen other instruments for this phase of Reformation history. Luther himself always saw it in that light. Though he often expressed his restless impatience, he felt himself throughout the proceedings at one with his associates who braved the heat of the battle, particularly with his intimate friend, Melanchthon.

---

[1] It is worth while to ponder what this ban meant for Luther. Even if it could not be rigidly enforced, because the otherwise very cautious Elector of Saxony refused to yield his principles, Luther was in constant danger, and an attempt on his life would have probably gone unpunished. It meant, at the least, that throughout his life Luther never enjoyed a sense of civic security. His writings still show that they were not composed in an atmosphere of quietness and relaxation.

Hero worship and the corresponding depreciation of those who do not seem to measure up to our standards of a "hero" are not the prerogative only of simple minds; one finds them occasionally even among scholars. Melanchthon's position at Augsburg has frequently been misunderstood. It is stated that cautious negotiations and diplomatic maneuvers now prevailed in place of the firm courage that had marked Luther's stand at Worms.

Two comments seem to be in order. Luther never entertained this opinion about Melanchthon. It is true that he attempted by correspondence to instill faith and courage in his timid, hesitant friend. Some of Luther's greatest letters date from this period. But one must not misread these letters as expressions of criticism when they were actually meant as encouragement. They disclose, in fact, one aspect of Luther's truly great personality. Without questions or misgivings he respected his friend's individuality. His famous remark about the Augsburg Confession dare not be misunderstood. After tedious political and theological conferences, Melanchthon drafted the final form in his precise, stately Latin style. Luther commented: "I have read Magister Philip's Apologia. I am well pleased with it and would not know how I could improve it. Furthermore, it would not be right because I cannot step so softly and carefully." That was not irony but wholehearted praise for a friend and his labors. Luther's final estimate of the outcome is as positive as possible. When he thought back to this diet, he was always grateful "that the Word was preserved and we with the Word."

From the start of the negotiations Melanchthon made every effort to prevent the schism from becoming permanent. He put great emphasis upon the phraseology of the imperial summons "to hear the well-intentioned opinions and ideas of everyone." The whole strength of his theological argument

rests upon the assertion that the Evangelicals had not established a new church. His first intention had been to discuss
only ecclesiastical abuses and their correction. The obstinacy
of his opponents, who wished to extend the debate to a discussion of dogmatic differences, finally forced him to deal
with articles of faith and doctrine. In this manner did the
Augsburg Confession become the classical document of
Protestantism.

Similar considerations had prompted the Elector John the
Constant, Frederick's successor, to present the work of Melanchthon and his friends as nothing more than the opinion
of the Duchy of Saxony. Only by great effort did the other
princes and estates finally obtain permission to add their sig-
natures and thereby give the document the character of an
official declaration of faith. The tactics of the opposition
forced the Evangelicals to demand an opportunity for a public declaration of their beliefs. Their determination brought
it about, that on June 25, 1530, the Confession was solemnly
read before the emperor and the princes. The opponents,
rather than the Evangelicals themselves, created the situation
by which the *Augustana* became the first official declaration
of the evangelical faith.

Melanchthon's frequently criticized conduct reflects great
credit upon the Reformers. They tried to the very end to
preserve the Christian unity of the Western world. It must
also be pointed out that Luther was in complete agreement
with Melanchthon. In only one respect did they hold differ-
ing opinions. Luther was certain that this unity could no
longer be saved and his historical judgment proved the more
accurate. The disruption of the Christian community weighed
more heavily upon Melanchthon than Luther. The humanist
treasured the great common European heritage but Luther
called that "a worldly care." He felt that if it was God's will

to lead his church into such calamity, God would also pre-serve it, whatever outward forms it might have to take in the future. A superficial reading of the *Augustana* fails to do justice to the preciseness and lucidity of its theological formu-lations.

The article on the office of preaching, for instance, in which the hierarchical order of the Catholic Church is re-jected, remains valid to this day. The last article deals with the power of the bishops. Moderate in language, it offers a clear concept of the separation of spiritual and secular powers which has lost none of its relevancy by the passing of time.

Luther in the meantime was not idle in Coburg. His rest-less spirit chafed under this enforced privacy and he com-plained, groundlessly in fact, that his friends failed to keep him informed. One can understand this feeling, as one can understand his many attempts to contribute something of his own toward strengthening the faith of his friends at Augs-burg. His letters to them are inspiring documents of Chris-tian confidence and courage.

Two days before his departure from Coburg, October 2, 1530, he summarized his feelings about the diet in a sermon. The emperor and the estates had rejected the Confession, and the emperor had even refused to accept the Apologia which was intended to defend the Confession against the objections of the Catholic party. But the young Lutheran Church was no longer in need of protection. Luther could declare in his sermon, "If they wish to be friendly toward us, let them be so in God's name. If not, they do not have to be, we do not care. The heaven is greater than the earth and things will probably not be turned upside down in such a way that the earth will rule the heavens. If they are plotting against us, they must first ask the Lord God for his approval. If he does not want it, let them scheme and plan as much as they wish, it is written: He that sitteth in the heavens shall laugh. The Lord shall have them in derision. . . . He shall vex them in his sore displeasure. For he is the God who created the world out of nothing, who quickeneth the dead and calleth those things which be not as though they were" (Rom. 4:17).

The world of men and things is a world of many uncertainties. True faith, as Luther stated so majestically, must learn "to stand upon the Nothing." God, who has called all his works out of the void, is mightier than all earthly might.

History has vindicated Luther's confidence.

Schmalkalden

The council occupied the same position of supreme authority in the Christian world which the diet occupied in the public life of the nation. Luther had frequently criticized the councils and denied their infallibility. It was good judgment on his part to suspend this criticism for the time being and join with other Protestant leaders in the demand that a council should be convoked immediately. Such a gathering offered the only possibility to effect a "reform of head and members," if such reform was really wanted. By insistent appeals Luther finally forced the papacy to state its position. There may have been various reasons why individual popes shunned these requests; the ultimate reason was secret fear. The more shallow popes practiced delays, always the easiest device for avoiding a decision. It did not further the cause of a council that it became a pawn in the game of high European politics. Charles V sincerely favored it; Francis I and Henry VIII were usually opposed to it. Not only the papacy but Christianity itself suffered irreparable harm by this policy of procrastination. The long delay was one of the chief reasons why the break became incurable.

Paul III, who had ascended the papal throne in 1533, finally agreed to call a council, and after the usual postponements it was definitely summoned to meet in Mantua at Pentecost in the year 1537. There can be no doubt that Paul III, worldly as he was and busily engaged in securing feudal estates for his children and grandchildren, was sincere in his desire for a council. A very odd circumstance proves it. In order to learn how the German princes felt about a council, he sent his *nuntius,* Paolo Vergerio, to Germany. The papal delegate arrived in Wittenberg in November and was pleasantly surprised to learn that the Elector was not at home. He extended an invitation to Luther and Bugenhagen to have dinner with him at the electoral palace. Luther accepted in a mood of grim humor. "Look at us, riding here," he joked on his way to the palace. "Here come the German pope and Cardinal Bugenhagen." It was his first encounter with a papal official after the Diet at Worms. By now, Luther was sure of himself and met the *nuntius* with firmness, made no concessions, and expressed doubt that the pope was sincere in his plans for a council. Vergerio, an experienced, judicious, and moderate man, who later embraced Protestantism himself, thought at first that Luther was "possessed," and the meeting produced no results. But preparations for the council progressed and in December the Elector instructed Luther "to state his grounds and meanings from the Holy Scriptures, as he would at the hour of his death expect to stand and endure before the judgment seat of almighty God."

Luther began immediately with this task and stayed with it even during an attack of illness, when he was only able to dictate. After final consultations with Melanchthon, Bugenhagen, and others, he presented the completed articles to the Elector on January 3, 1537. Four days later he received this remarkable reply:

"May the almighty God grant grace to all of us through our Lord Jesus Christ that we may abide in constant true faith and that no fear of men and their opinions may sway us.

"To the extent that this involves risks and dangers for our lands and subjects or individuals, we commit it unto God's keeping, for he has said that the very hairs on our heads are all numbered (Matt. 10:30) and we shall lose none of them without his divine will. The same God will order all matters growing out of this danger as far as it concerns our brother, ourselves, and our children, land, and people and we want to leave everything in his care. He has chosen us to be a prince. If he wants it otherwise, no caution of ours will do any good, for he will do as he pleases."

Strangely enough, Luther could no more attend the Council of Schmalkalden, where the articles were debated, than he had been able to attend the Diet at Augsburg. As soon as he arrived in town, he became seriously ill. Johann Mathesius reports that he asked to be removed from Schmalkalden. "He commended his soul, praying the church's prayer and made a brief Christian confession. He would abide by the Lord Jesus Christ and his Word, knew in his heart no other righteousness than the precious blood of Christ which, by grace alone, could cleanse him and all believers . . . He also made his last will and testament in the carriage." His associates expected his death momentarily. The Elector who had given Luther as much assistance as he could, considered the illness so critical that he notified Frau Käthe to meet them on the way, for it was not expected that her husband would reach home alive. Luther himself felt that his end was near. *"Summa,* I was dead, and committed you and the child into God's keeping," he wrote from Tambach on February 27, after his condition had suddenly improved during the night.

In that same night he wrote a very cordial letter to Melanchthon, telling of the wonderful change, in which he saw God's answer to the many prayers of his friends. "This example ought to teach us to pray and hope that help will come from above." His friends thought so also, and when Luther's young companion, Magister Schlaginhauffen, arrived in

Schmalkalden at dawn on February 28, he announced jubilantly, *"Lutherus vivit!* (Luther is alive.)"

Meanwhile Melanchthon's advice had prevailed that the Evangelicals should rest their case on the Augsburg Confession and the Apologia. The term "Schmalkald Articles" is really a misnomer. They were actually never discussed or endorsed by the Protestants in attendance at the council. This was not meant as a compromise. Melanchthon had been authorized to state anew the Protestant attitude towards the papacy. He had done it in the famous *Tractatus de potestate papae,* which he completed on February 17. This essay proves once more that Melanchthon stood firm in all matters that involved a principle. The delegates of pope and emperor had made a futile journey; they had to return without having achieved their purpose. It was largely their own fault. They had definite instructions to act pleasantly and conciliatorily but thought they could gain more by assuming a brusque and haughty demeanor. Unwittingly, as often happens in history, they saved the young Lutheran Church from entanglements and the compromise of its principles. Not until the council had adjourned did the theologians, following a suggestion of Bugenhagen, sign the articles as individuals.

Luther's articles therefore failed to influence the course of events directly, particularly since the council adjourned indefinitely after three previous interruptions. Only after an interval of eight years did it meet again in Trent in 1545. But the indirect influence was great indeed. In some respects the Articles of Schmalkalden are the most lucid, most perfect of the Lutheran confessions because they are of one piece. Since they were not submitted to modifications at a conference table, they retained their original form and are the most intimate expression of Luther's own faith incorporated in the *Book of Concord,* that collection of Lutheran confessions which was compiled in 1580 in observance of the fiftieth anniversary of the Diet at Worms.

The Articles of Schmalkalden embody two very important conclusions. They accept the separation as an accomplished fact. After a searching analysis of all existing differences, Luther reasoned that history itself had created the break and that it was impossible to reverse the process. "Thus we are separated and thus we shall remain forever."

A very sensitive criterion of the religious life reveals how deep the gulf really was. Luther saw in contemporary Catholicism the richest flower and perfection of natural religion. As such it differs fundamentally from the faith that is evoked by the gospel. He coined the term "enthusiasm" for this kind of natural religiosity. It is the religious ardor of man. It does not produce a break with one's self, a sense of self-effacement, but constitutes in the realm of religion the highest form of self-assertion.

"Enthusiasm inheres in Adam and his children from the beginning to the end of the world, put there, and poisoned by the old dragon . . . and is the origin, strength, and power of all heresy. Therefore we ought to and must insist that God is not willing to deal with us humans, except through his external word and sacrament."

In the language of the sixteenth century "external word" connotes a word that comes from without, one that man could not utter himself. It is not an inner voice, not a religious need, not the spiritual yearning of the human soul, but the revealed Word that God himself pronounces in his majesty.

Luther discerns and rejects the element of natural religion in the three religious systems of his age. The "spiritualists" represent the mystics of all times. The Catholic Church is the prototype of work-righteousness. Islam stands for all forms of rationalism.

It is as if Luther had anticipated the most dangerous attack upon all religion: Feuerbach's assertion that religion is ultimately a form of self-deception. Luther's faith in the revealed Word of God can never be reconciled with the many types of religious humanism current in our day. It is as sharply opposed to any kind of racial mysticism as to romantic hero worship, or scientific positivism, or any of the other pseudo religions that are in vogue today.

A stroke of genius enabled Luther to draw a clear line of demarkation between biblical faith and "enthusiasm."

The Bequest

On February 18, 1546, Luther closed his eyes in Eisleben, the same city where he had first opened them to the light of day sixty-three years before. A circle of wide circumference was thus closed—a childhood in the home of a miner and small independent contractor, academy and university, monastery and professorship, Worms, Augsburg, Schmalkalden, and always Wittenberg. Luther's career had no equal in his day.

The Saale and Elbe rivers were at flood stage when Luther started on his journey to Mansfeld in the immediate vicinity of his birthplace. The counts of Mansfeld had invited him to serve as arbitrator in a family dispute. It was late in January and Luther was by this time a tired and sick man. He did not wish to decline a request that came to him from his childhood community, but he started on the journey with grave misgivings. The wearisome travel in the dead of winter was a great hardship. An ice-cold wind blew on him and caused him agonizing headaches; he felt very ill by the time he arrived in Mansfeld, where an honor guard of 113 mounted soldiers awaited him. After some rest his condition improved. But besides the unpleasant negotiations he was kept busy with sermons, ordinations, communions, and demands for personal counsel and advice.

In the evening hours of February 17 he suffered an acute attack of an ailment that had troubled him for some time.

His customary remedies gave him some relief, but the attack recurred in the morning hours of February 18 and this time was accompanied by great weakness. His friends realized the seriousness of his condition and summoned a physician and the two princes. His attendants tried in vain to preserve the fading spark of life. His prayers were still audible and his friend Justus Jonas recorded them. "O my heavenly Father, God and Father of our Lord Jesus Christ, Thou God of all comfort, I thank Thee that Thou hast revealed Thy dear Son Jesus Christ to me, in whom I believe, whom I have confessed and proclaimed, whom the wicked pope and all unbelievers malign, persecute and blaspheme. I pray Thee, my Lord Jesus Christ, accept my soul. Heavenly Father, though I must leave this body and be snatched out of this world, I know that I shall abide with Thee forever and that no one can pluck me out of Thy hands." Several times he prayed the sentence from the *Completorium:* Into Thy hands I commend my spirit, Thou gracious God.

When he had lapsed into silence, his two most faithful friends and co-workers called to him: "Reverend Father, are you willing to die confidently in the belief in Christ and his doctrine as you have preached it?" He replied with a clear "yes" and soon "he passed away peacefully and calmly as Simeon sings."

The accounts which appeared immediately after his death indicate that Luther's contemporaries were fully aware of the fact that a great life had come to an end. Yet they could not possibly fathom the multitude of impressions which the memory of that day conveys to us.

The man who died at Eisleben, almost 25 years after the events of Worms, was no longer the popular hero of his earlier days or the honored central figure in a world-wide movement. It could even look as though his life had settled down to the commonplace. He had aged and become corpulent, and he was frequently troubled by physical ailments. It was not a pleasant world in which he had to live, and life brought him, as it did others, more disappointments than fulfilled hopes.

The last chapters of the Reformation appear drab, cloaked in such undistinguished resignation that their impact upon modern consciousness is almost lost, and even scholars have turned away from the "old Luther" who seems no longer attractive or inspiring. The impression is false. It would be far more correct to state that the "old Luther" was great because he lived to his last day by the same truth he had always taught, namely, that God justifies the sinner. What made his last years great was the sober realism and unfailing clarity with which he judged men and events, without falling into resignation, despondency, or fear.

That applies also to the political scene. Unlike most other Germans, he had no time for political daydreams. He was, as a rule, skeptical of the emperor and his policies, even when they seemed to favor him. He was one of the few men who perceived clearly that the game of European power politics played into the hands of the most dangerous common foe: the Turks. He was annoyed at the German and European princes who pursued their petty dynastic wars as though this great threat to the Christian world were nonexistent. At times he berated them with caustic irony, at other times he warned them in solemn earnestness. We have his writings on the Turkish threat to thank for many of his most important fundamental ideas on politics—ideas which are to be found in these works.

His instructions for church administration are equally realistic. They are devoid of the emotional fervor of the "enthusiasts." The fact that since the order for the visitation of parishes in 1529, Luther continued to stress the need for religious education, proves that he held no illusions about the human beings with whom he had to deal. They were not the advance guard of the *communio sanctorum* but illiterate, stolid individuals in need of instruction and preaching. He was thus saved from that bias which uncritically rejects or condemns people. Human contacts always filled him with a mingled sense of joy and pain. He often reminded his hearers that the orderly instruction of youth bears fruit and displeases the devil. He admonished parents, teachers, and magistrates to discharge their duties toward the next generation faithfully. But all the while he was certain that the world will not be changed as if by magic as soon as the Word of God is proclaimed, but that the gospel message and Satan will contend until the end of time.

When he felt that even his own city, Wittenberg, was not really sanctified by the Word of God, when citizens and students persevered in their old ways, Luther decided suddenly to move away. He did not wish to stay in a place where people were so little inclined to heed the Word of God. The city fathers became thoroughly alarmed at the prospect of losing their most distinguished citizen under such humiliating circumstances and put forth great efforts, until Luther finally agreed to return. One is immediately reminded of Calvin's strict reign in Geneva, which gave that city during his lifetime the appearance of a Christian community.

But was Luther on this account the lesser of the two men? Even Calvin could not safeguard Geneva against the later influence of Rousseau. Is there, furthermore, any social order of which we can say that it is in complete harmony with the gospel? Was not Luther in reality the more consistent, because, as a teacher and preacher of the gospel, he refused firmly to avail himself of any means but the Word of God?

That was his principle in all matters pertaining to the organization of churches. He was not a pedantic official, determined to regulate every trivial detail of life, but wanted much rather to see indigenous growth as long as it did not harm the gospel. Let us state it plainly: Luther was not at home in an atmosphere of rigorous legalism; his ethics reflected the forgiving grace of God in man's everday activities. No earthly order will ever completely actualize God's holy will. That ideal can only be realized in the world beyond, but meanwhile we must live in a world in which the sun rises upon the just and unjust. He who recognizes his own need for daily divine forgiveness will also recognize those areas in public life where we owe each other forebearance and forgiveness. Luther would never have fitted into a totalitarian system, because he could not think in terms of an inflexible doctrinairism. It is this very rigidity which makes dealings with dictators of all types so unsatisfactory.

The breadth of vision which always characterizes true genius is in Luther's case coupled with a faith in God who by grace alone prevents the world from slipping into chaos. It is a distortion to portray the "old Luther" as a disgruntled, disappointed individual. He was fully aware of the one factor which preserves life and society in an imperfect world and among failing men.

It is, therefore, a wrong deduction to assume that the "old Luther" no longer upheld the theology of his youth. His theology never changed, for he never advocated any other theology than the *theologia crucis.* The theology of the cross was the core of his testimony, sanctified by sober thinking, enlarged by his eschatological expectation. Anguish remains a characteristic mark of a genuine Christian existence, as persecution and oppression are the stigmata of a true church. But the individual Christian and the church walk only in the way the Master has walked before them, the way of the Passion. Over and beyond all vicissitudes of life waits that eternal destiny, the great day of God, toward which all events of history move. It is not a tired, fatalistic, narrow view of history but a majestic vision of a universal destiny.

Neither is it true that Luther's theological productivity decreased during these later years, either in quantity or incisiveness of thought. His most elaborate course of lectures, the exegesis of Genesis, was offered during the last decade of his life. In this respect Luther resembled Titian, or the aged Goethe who, toward the end of his life, worked on the second part of his *Faust*. These men made their greatest contributions in their old age. Luther now had an opportunity to set forth the nature of revelation, the biblical concept of the meaning of human existence, and the significance of the fear of death in an evangelical doctrine of the nature of man.

Best of all, his theology and his Christian life merge into one during these latter years. The powerful "yes" by which he affirmed his whole theological work in his dying hour had also been the guiding principle of his everyday life. He is *simul iustus et peccator*, simultaneously sinner and just man. God's justification of the sinner becomes the fundamental motive of his life. That is what makes the aging Luther so undramatic. He had a clear notion of his place in history and occasionally alluded to it without false modesty. But he lived toward the last without a trace of affectation. Unlike the aged Goethe who wrapped himself in a cloak of unapproachable, imposing dignity, Luther remained a common man in friendliness and anger, in earnestness and play, in his realism and in his faith.

He kept his remarkable courage toward the last. A man who suffered as much physical pain as he did, who constantly saw his life work threatened by powerful opponents, could easily have become subject to moods of severe depression. But he often stated that all the enemies of the gospel are ultimately helpless. "He who is with us, is stronger than he who is in the world." Christ is mightier than Satan. *"Christus Satana major."* A note which was found after his death, and contains his last written words, reads like a summary of his life work. "Nobody can understand Vergil's bucolics who has not himself herded sheep for five years; nobody can understand Cicero, unless he has been active for twenty-five years in public affairs. Nobody has a right to assume he has tasted enough of the Scriptures, unless he has ruled the congregation for one hundred years with prophets like Elias and Elisha, John the Baptist, Christ, and the apostles. Do not tempt these divine *Aeneases* but bow adoringly before what they have done! We are beggars, that is true."

That is, of course, the very antithesis to the modern approach. During the last two centuries the theory of man's autonomy has become established. Today no one doubts that this rebellion has reached a stalemate. The individual, who has become the measure of all things, begins to doubt himself; he has become homeless in the very universe he wished to rule without God and eternal constraint.

In the face of all our achievements which have ultimately turned into weapons of destruction, Luther and his last reverberating words are still right: "We are beggars, that is true."

Fundamentally, of course, the important fact is not that we are beggars; important is Luther's faith in God who is the hope of the lowly, the comfort of the sinner, the life of the dying, and the One who fills the empty hands of the beggar.

Part III

The Heritage

The statement that a new epoch in history originated in the purely religious experience of the man, Luther, and that the impact of this experience has extended to this day, sounds so fantastic that one hesitates to accept it. Yet our very reluctance may be symptomatic of the illness of our age. At any rate, it is worth while to examine the reasons for our skepticism.

For one thing, many of us no longer have any conception of the basic, personal decision by which one abides in life or death. We are reaping the harvest of two centuries of tolerance, once a great and noble cause which meant respect for all that constitutes the dignity of man. In time, however, the concept became so broadened, so devoid of all real content, that today it signifies little more than the toleration of trivial, personal differences of opinion. It is not generally realized that, in the process of popularizing toleration, we have sacrificed respect for the dignity of man. There can be no true tolerance unless there are basic, uncompromising convictions, come what may. Where such convictions have ceased to exist, the dignity of man has disappeared. Our generation can tolerate many shades of opinion because they are no longer vital to us; they are varied convictions which are readily interchangeable. The most ominous sign of our spiritual disintegration is the intellectual flexibility which enables men to submit without any great inward struggle to officially endorsed points of view. Decisions by which one risks everything, even death, have become rare. The only exceptions in our day seem to be the political martyrs. We have seen men in the recent past who were ready to suffer death for their political convictions, though their number is probably smaller than one would assume.

Religious convictions belong in a different category, largely because religion itself has ceased to influence cultural trends to any appreciable extent during the past century. A paradoxical situation has thereby arisen. There have been numerous martyrs in the church, shining examples of faithfulness unto death, particularly among groups at the edge of official Christianity.[1] The members of certain sects have faced imprisonment and death with a fortitude and devotion reminiscent of the early days of the church. But religion has become such an isolated element in the intellectual life of the times that the general public has been hardly aware of these events.

As a result, the last two generations no longer even realize that human existence can only be established in faith. This metaphysical impoverishment has gone so far that we look with extreme distrust upon all manifestations of a personal religious faith and are really no longer capable of understanding such a phenomenon. The aforementioned, unprincipled, intellectual submissiveness is the most characteristic mark of this decline. It is a tragic fate that the century which fought so valiantly to gain autonomy for the individual finally ended by enmeshing him in a new servitude which has no

---

[1] Luther, incidentally was in the same position. He did not become a martyr, but seen from the secular historian's point of view that is sheer coincidence. In his situation he had to count on such a possibility at all times. He was fully conscious of this danger after he had publicly burned the bull of excommunication. Immediately after this act, he began a course of lectures in which he publicly mentioned the possibility of his death by violence.

equal in history. These are the reasons why the claim that modern history begins with Luther's personal religious experience sounds at first so incredible—but in developing the difference between the faith of the Reformation and the metaphysical exhaustion of our present philosophies of life, we are already indicating the promise which the heritage of the Reformation holds out to us.

The Faith

A careful analysis of Luther's work and way through life makes it very evident that his personal experience of the faith is indeed the decisive factor which has been the source of his influence upon succeeding generations. In his case the man and his work become as one. It can be stated without exaggeration that no other occidental thinker has been quite so sensitive to the intensely personal element in human existence as Luther. His thought is organized around the concept of man as an individual and begins with the recognition of the loneliness in which man appears before God at the moment of death. Luther expressed this most clearly in his introduction to the so-called Invocavit sermons of 1522.[1]

He preached them in Wittenberg after he had left the safety of his Wartburg refuge, in an attempt to bring the riotous excesses of the "enthusiasts" to an end.

He said: "Death claims all of us and every one must die for himself. I cannot be with you, and you cannot be with me. We may shout into each other's ears but each man must stand on the ramparts alone."

Two truths are expressed in this terse statement. There is, first, the fact that there is a Lord over life. Though the idea is not explicitly mentioned in the introduction, it is developed

---

[1] These sermons are preserved in two versions. The text quoted above retains the essential features of both accounts. They do not differ in content.

further in the sermon; it is so characteristic of Luther's thought that it dare not be overlooked.

Luther's awareness of man's isolation in the hour of death is by no means identical with modern individualism. Individualism is the ripest fruit of autonomy, the notion that man is his own master and therefore also lord over his own life. Such a viewpoint simply does not exist for Luther. As long as man is alive, he may entertain the delusion that his fate rests in his own hands. At the last, at the moment of death, this belief is shattered, because dying itself constitutes an inescapable limitation that is imposed upon us from without. Christ once reminded us pointedly that we cannot add a fraction to our allotted life span. This fact, which death makes unmistakably clear, should be remembered by man all his life.

One misinterprets human nature if one forgets that there is a Master who controls man, not only in death but in life.

Another aspect is more important in this connection: no one can take our place at the moment of dying, every man dies his own death. But it is one of man's deep-rooted tendencies to seek substitutes. The ideal of a "hero," who is oblivious of the present and future, always obedient to the dictates of duty, always ready to accept every responsibility that falls to his lot, is a figment of the imagination, unconfirmed by the experiences of everyday life.

By and large, men are always grateful for those who relieve them of decisions and responsibilities. One of the deadly ills of our modern world is the growing disinclination to make responsible ethical decisions. In its place we find the frightening compliance in the realm of fundamental ethical choices which every individual must make. So it has come about that even highly intelligent people have promptly surrendered basic decisions which affect the upbringing of their own children, the relationship of free men to their government, their faith, their nation, their families. They have renounced their rights to determine these matters themselves, much less to offer resistance on moral grounds.[2]

There is one point, however, at which this tendency to make substitutions breaks down—at the moment of death. Dying is the most intensely personal of all human experiences, because at the moment of death we enter into the presence of God. All the materialist theories of the last one hundred and fifty years have not been able to destroy man's deep intuition that death is more than a biological process. The cessation of cellular function is perhaps the least significant factor. Man is ordinarily quite aware of the fact that death is no trifling matter, but that it is the great mystery of life. It is GOD who lets us die. At the moment of death only two personalities are everlastingly important, God and I. This is the unutterable loneliness of man. At that moment no one can take his place. Perhaps it is the first time that he has really come face to face with God.

This insight, however, is not limited to the death experience for death casts a reflected light upon the whole life that has preceded it. That position constitutes a fundamental concept in Reformation thinking. What is true of death is just as true of life. No one can substitute for us. We cannot trade existence with anyone else. As no one can die as our representative, so no one can live as our representative. In this life also, we are face to face with God and no one can take our place. God addresses himself to man not only in

---

[2] For the diagnosis it matters little whether we submit to the whim of a dictator or "public opinion." (The author uses the English term.) While they differ greatly in details, the essentials remain the same. It is equally besides the point, whether one dresses one's surrender up by calling it "duty" or "loyalty," or whether one cynically admits the facts, or is sufficiently indifferent not to think about them at all.

the hour of death, but throughout life. Man becomes God's partner and that relationship demands a response and responsibility from us. Those who know nothing of this responsibility can never rightfully claim any dignity for man. A truly ethical existence can only rest upon this recognition of responsibility, upon the awareness that man lives his life in the presence of God. All the eloquent references to the moral law within us, to duty (whatever that may mean or how it may change from generation to generation) or, worse yet, to the "voice of the blood," are shallow and secularized substitutes.

It would be premature, however, to assume immediately that the gulf between modern and Reformation thought is insurmountable. "God moves in a mysterious way," and our generation is about to rediscover the impressive truth that no one can take the individual's place before God. The idea that man is a creature who is comfortably adjusted to a finite universe belongs to the past. The theories of man as a self-directed, adequate human being are gradually replaced by a sense of life's dreadfulness, and philosophers have recently described it in metaphors of unforgettable grandeur. Nowhere else has the human situation been subjected to such searching analyses as in these modern philosophies. "The roof of the world has been taken off" and infinity looks in again, in all its awesomeness. These are the words of Professor Karl Jaspers. Man is no longer a superior creature who stands in front or even above his fate; he now trembles before the terrifying question how he can bear his own existence in the world. "The dread of existence" (Jaspers) is the most characteristic modern reaction to life, a dread "which is fearful of existence itself" (Heidegger).

A man who has felt this anxiety concerning life cannot be the complacent citizen of the world, of whom Kierkegaard

115

said that "he dwells satisfied and secure in the finite." This modern man is, to say the least, disquieted by one overwhelming question, that of existence itself. He is therefore more likely to take cognizance of Luther's answer to this fundamental question.

The Reformers were profoundly conscious of man's inability to live by himself before God. As soon as God addresses him, man feels his obligation to respond and thereby to become responsible; yet he finds at that very moment that he cannot make that response and assume that responsibility by his own strength. He discovers that he breaks down before the absolute demands that God makes of him.

It is a basic insight of the Reformers that God grants existence before him as a gift which man cannot realize by himself.

This forms the background for the evangelical doctrine of the justification of the sinner. At the precise moment when God summons man, man becomes conscious of his existential guilt. We must not understand this guilt in any moralistic sense as a series of trespasses, but as the total human inability to live up to the divine demand. Yet in spite of our guilt and inadequacy God permits us to live before him. The existential dread of man is well founded, for he cannot live in this world by his own competence. Yet the dread is removed immediately because man lives a privileged existence in the life that God bestows upon him through Christ.

We can now understand why this basic orientation toward life is not one of fear or despair, though it acknowledges the fearsomeness of death and man's total guilt before God. Evangelical piety is essentially a sense of joy. It is reflected in the rich hymnody and preaching of the times and it is shared by all teachers of the church, no matter how much they might otherwise differ among themselves. The "dread

116

of existence" has lost its sting because fear of hell and death, anguish of conscience, and remorse over sin no longer exercise their power. Life has become possible once more.

We must yet examine how this new insight has affected the concept of the church, but we can see immediately that it was diametrically opposed to the pernicious trend which made of the church a hierarchical institution.

There was no longer any room for the mediating services of persons or rituals. We can also understand Luther's feeling that the Catholic Church of his day had committed treason against the true church. It had endeavored to "relieve" man of his existence in the immediate presence of God. Luther raised exactly the objections against the Church of Rome which Dostoevski voiced later in *The Grand Inquisitor.*

We notice the importance of this orientation toward a new philosophy of life and man. The individual existence of man has now become possible and thereby real. It consists in that personal responsibility which every man bears before God. Before we investigate this phase we must first call attention to another important aspect of the faith of the Reformers. This faith may be compared to an ellipse with two focal points. The one is the recognition that no one can substitute for the individual before God; the other is the fact that it is God who addresses himself to the individual. This relationship is frequently described by two rather colorless modern terms, subjectivism and objectivism.[3] They are, however, unfortunate and misleading misnomers.

---

[3] The claim that one can distinguish between the "objective" piety of the Reformation period and the "subjective" piety of a later period should be discarded as historically and factually erroneous. The great Reformation hymn, "Rejoice dear Christians with one accord," begins in nine out of ten stanzas with the personal pronoun. Psychologically, a life which in some of its aspects is not altogether subjective is impossible; a wholly objective life is fortunately inconceivable.

The evangelical understanding of the newly given life rests upon the conviction that we are not dealing with subjective processes of cognition, or emotion, or moral effort. This new existence has really been made available to man from without by the Lord and Creator of life himself. It is not the end result of man's philosophizing, but an event. Something has happened to him that is dependent upon God's revelation.

This, like so many of Luther's truly great new insights, is only incidentally expressed in his writings. In the lectures on Genesis, he refers to the assertion of St. Paul that an eternal momentum is released in man, once he has been called by God. As God in the beginning called out into darkness, "Let there be light," so God now addresses himself creatively to man, "Let there be light," and it brings forth "the light of the knowledge of the glory of God in the face of Jesus Christ" (II Cor. 4:6).

Only at that moment, which represents another aspect of the singularly vigorous evangelical view of man, can man become a human being in the fullest sense of the word. A man without faith possesses biological existence and possibly additional characteristics, but not until he has harkened to the voice of God has he achieved true humanity.

This call by God reaches us in various ways. It occurs fundamentally in Jesus Christ. In Christ God has addressed himself to all mankind, has spoken to men in time and space by introducing Christ into the arena of human history. (The "history" of Jesus includes his miracles, particularly the resurrection, as genuine events.) This call of God, which was principally issued through Christ, is continued in our testimony of him. Where Christ is preached in faith and accepted in faith, he is present, whether this testimony takes the form of a quotation from St. Paul, or a hymn, or the Catechism, or any other of the various types of proclamations of Christ.

God's call is therefore not a single, completed, petrified event in the past but a recurrent process, which began during the earthly ministry of Christ and has continued to this day.[4] The proclamation of Christ is a present reality. It will continue and remain alive, because God is the Creator and Lord of life.[5]

The church, the vessel of the Word, dare never become institutionalized but must always remain a creative power. The fact that Christ is proclaimed makes the church; nothing else does.

In the opinion of the Reformers no complete human exisence is possible unless that faith is realized. Herein lies the greatest contribution which the Reformation can make to present-day thinking. It can say something that cannot be said by anyone else or in any other way.

The cynicism of the first two decades of the century and the feverish creation of pseudo religions which we have witnessed during the last thirty years are indications that an era is approaching its end. It is no longer the age of a self-assured, earthbound generation, so sure in its sense of superiority that it has become a stranger to the gospel. It is a generation that is weary from its long journey through un-

---

[4] If Lagarde calls the relationship of the believing Christian to the historical event a form of fetishism "with the single exception, that the object of worship is not a natural but historical phenomenon," he merely displays his misunderstanding of the essential factor. The singular historical event becomes a present reality through the preaching of the Word. One may also state it like this: Lagarde knew nothing of the third article of the Creed or the work of the Holy Spirit.

[5] It is not the mechanically understood Word of the Scriptures to which man owes his faith, but the Word that has become lucid in the light of the justification. "Biblicists" existed before Luther. All religious reformers and reform movements since Wycliffe have appealed to the Bible. The difference lies in the new understanding that Luther brought to the study of the Word.

speakable suffering, and deeply anxious for guidance, wisdom, and truth. Humanity has grown perplexed, wondering whether it is still possible to draw a clear, untarnished picture of life and man.

It becomes the specific mission of Protestantism to provide the directives which grow out of its own understanding of the faith. This insight qualifies Protestantism to speak to this generation. Man's existence is ultimately grounded in faith, and only within that faith can life's potentialities be realized. It is essential that this faith should prove itself in times of great inner stress. In Luther's own case the forces of history provided the test. He kept his faith intact, even under the threat of death. We, who are accustomed to the protection of the law, can scarcely realize what it must have meant for Luther to live the rest of his life under the ban of the empire. On some occasions, particularly in 1518 and 1521, he faced the very real possibility of death at the stake.

His spiritual suffering was equally severe. It was a struggle against death and Satan. The spiritual conflict, in fact, predominated. Luther found out that vital faith is always attended by temptation. He passed through all the fires of doubt, particularly doubt in God. It did not take the pale form of modern agnosticism, but the much more terrifying doubt whether God had forsaken him or no longer cared about this man, Martin Luther. In the agonies of his soul he anticipated the great theme of the spiritual history of the West which reached its climax in Nietzsche. The most dynamic issue which ever challenged the spirituality of the West is essentially already present. One cannot but feel that all later formulations are only slight repetitions, humanistic variations of a theme that Luther had already known in all its power and dreadfulness. Herein lies our hope. Ours is a generation that has been driven into the abyss of despair, sorrowed by death and horror, tortured by the question whether God is still discernible in this demon-ridden world.

In Luther's world view, faith is the core of religion. It is not an embellishment but a necessity of life, more indispensable than breath itself.

The Church

The same problem that has concerned us throughout this whole inquiry comes before us once more. We have attempted to show that the so-called modern era in history begins as the personal religious experience of one man. As such, however, it occurs within the framework of the organized church. The era that came to be known as the modern age begins as an event in church history, the formation of a new ecclesiastical body. Modern man finds this almost incomprehensible. It is difficult though not impossible for him to realize that the modern age had its incipience in a religious experience. It is almost impossible for him to understand that it began over the question of "The Church."

When we speak of church, we mean, of course, the church of Jesus Christ; as by faith we do not mean just any faith or one of the countless varieties of religion, but a specific faith—the faith in Jesus Christ.

Though we may count on a certain degree of understanding on the part of modern man when we speak of faith as a necessity of existence, we must not count on the same understanding when we speak of the church. This lack of comprehension makes it very difficult to show how much Luther can contribute to any modern view of the church.

Two conflicting interpretations seem to merge here. Many people think of themselves as loyal followers of Luther, because they credit him with the overthrow of ecclesiastical domination. By freeing all areas of life from the supreme authority of the church, he became the real father of the modern age. Devout Catholics meet this interpretation with the accusation that Luther destroyed the medieval church, or at least the unity of the church.

What, in the face of these claims and counterclaims, are the facts and their significance for the life of today?

We begin with the observation that for at least two decades the leaders of the Reformation, including Luther, never thought in terms of a new church. Though Luther had criticized the abuses of the church in some of his early lectures, he had done so strictly as a critic within the church. When he published the ninety-five theses on "the nature of indulgences," he offered for debate a subject which had not yet been "defined" by the church. It was therefore no dogma at the time and every Catholic theologian had the right to discuss it. He concluded all his disputations with the customary declaration that he had made no statement in violation of the official doctrines of the church or the authority of the pope. There is no evidence that Luther ever made this statement with any mental reservations or in sheer irony. The preface to one of his most important publications takes the form of an open letter to Pope Leo X. It is couched in respectful and pleading terms and there is no reason to doubt Luther's sincerity in the matter. His extreme positions were frequently forced upon him by the bullying tactics of his opponents. That was particularly true of the important debate at Leipzig, where Luther had to defend himself against the ambitious but shortsighted, blundering Eck.

It was significant that Luther should have chosen the garb of a monk when he suddenly and fearlessly appeared in Wittenberg on May 5, 1522, in order to squelch the rioting of the "Enthusiasts" by a series of sermons (the famous Invocavit sermons). He stood before these extremists as a monk rather than a "Junker Jörg." He still was tonsured, cleanly shaven, and garbed in the habit of an Augustinian friar, an attire which he retained until 1524. Not until 1525 did he marry Katharina von Bora.

The service of worship underwent only gradual revisions. The term "Protestants" was not used until 1529, and then it was invented by the opponents of the movement. Its first connotation was legal rather than doctrinal. The year 1530 brought the Diet of Augsburg and the Confession named after the city. It has often been claimed that the Confession, written by Melanchthon in the spirit and elegant Latin style of the humanists, deviates from Luther's position. Yet critical as Luther was of the proceedings, he never withheld his praise and approbation from the Confession itself. He was in full accord with the principle of showing that the Protestants were part of the old church. Melanchthon had taken his cue from the phraseology of the imperial summons and stated the gist of the Confession as demonstration *quod sub uno eodemque Christo sumus et militamus,* repeating word for word the statement of the emperor that "we are under the same Lord Christ and serve Him."

If the document appears conciliatory throughout, this restraint merely attests the eagerness to avoid the formation of a new church. Melanchthon's treatise *De Potestate et Primatu Papae* and the additions to the articles of Schmalkalden, which are incorporated in the Symbolical Books of the Lutheran Church, show such readiness to submit as no other evangelical church has ever shown again (Cf. Aug. 28; Ap. 24).

Only after the decisions at Augsburg had been reached did recognition gradually grow that the two groups could no longer remain within the bounds of one church.

The break became final during the winter 1537-38. Luther himself stated in the "Schmalkald Articles" that "we are and remain separated forever." But twenty years had passed since the publication of the ninety-five theses before he had come to this conclusion.

All this bears little resemblance to a revolt within the church or a deliberate attempt to set up a new church body. The uniqueness of Luther's attitude becomes particularly obvious when we compare it with that of the other leaders of the Reformation. Calvin offers the sharpest contrast. Unusually gifted in the formulation of ambitious programs and details of organization, he far surpassed Luther in these matters. Western Protestantism owes its leading position in the world to the character of Calvin and his genius for logical and purposeful planning. Calvin was the last of the great leaders of the Reformation who made their way independently of Luther. Zwingli was the first. He differed from Luther not only in the fact that he advocated a rationalistic-humanistic program of reform, but that he pursued clear-cut political aims in connection with the Reformation. Bolder, more determined to make the Reformation politically effective, he was also more flexible, more skillful, and infinitely more courageous than the man from Geneva.

Even more resolute was a group which stands chronologically between these two movements. It was a submerged, broad current of reformatory ideas which reached the surface among the anabaptists and other radical sects whom we usually designate by the collective term "enthusiasts." Here prevailed an intensity of feeling, a radical determination to achieve their aims which left the Lutheran Reformation far behind. Here we find the martyrs of the Reformation, here the Sermon on the Mount was taken literally without compromise or flinching. These groups scrapped the old traditions without hesitation and, if necessary, by force. With the courage of true confessors they attempted to order public life in conformity with the gospel, even at real sacrifices to themselves. They were the people who actually put many of Erasmus' ideals and suggestions for reform into practice. It cannot surprise us that some scholars have seen in them the truly consistent representatives of the Reformation spirit.

What did Rome do? Did the hierarchy realize at the time that a new church was coming into existence? Not at all. There were some astute observers like Eck in Ingolstadt, Cochlaeus in Frankfurt, Murner in Strasbourg who raised their voices in alarm. But since all of them were loud-mouthed, uncouth troublemakers, their own associates refused to take them seriously. For a long time the Renaissance popes were entirely unaware that a new church was in the making. They were busily engaged in the beautification of Rome. It was at this time that some of the most ornate and representative edifices which we associate with the name "Rome" were built. Much papal ingenuity and skill were devoted to the intricate tasks of administration and finances, but above all to politics, always to politics. It is one of the ironies of history that these political maneuvers were particularly aimed at the one great power which was ready to take firm measures against the Protestants—the House of Habsburg. For years the popes were unable to think of Luther as anything but a heretical monk. One is almost inclined to say that they saw him in the same light as Nietzsche and Lagarde in the nineteenth century: a boorish German monk "with a mind no broader than his wooden shoes."

For a whole generation, one pope after another closed his eyes to the fact that a reform movement was going on. When finally, after a long and disgraceful delay of three decades, the diet was called into session, the pope ignored the wishes of the emperor and made the doctrinal differences the first topic for discussion. By adopting binding decretals at the opening session, the papacy made the rift permanent from its side as well. No one else in the world had been as consistent in forcing Luther and his followers to form a new church as the men of the curia themselves. It was they who transformed the universal church of the Middle Ages into the confessional churches of the modern era.

Two facts are well established. Luther did not intend originally to establish a new church. His position can best be stated thus: The church, cleansed and restored by the Word of God, is the true successor to the church of St. Bernard, Francis of Assisi, and Thomas á Kempis. The Roman church having deviated from the course, the Evangelical church has found its way back to the true church of the Middle Ages.

It is equally wrong to assume that Luther wished to do away altogether with the concept of a church. The latter is the more dangerous of the two conceptions, because it is frequently stated as the typical Protestant position.

The deists of the eighteenth century looked upon the church as a form of human society in which the individual took part as far as he liked. The liberals of the nineteenth century were merely consistent when they contended that nobody needed to take part at all.

Goethe, who had been brought up in a vital Christian tradition and considered himself a Christian throughout most of his life, rarely attended a church service after he had attained manhood. Lagarde insisted vigorously that Protestantism had merely lacked the courage to draw the consequences from its own premises. Ever since the first world war, the influence of the church, both Catholic and Protestant, upon public life has gradually declined.

What we encounter here is the secularization of modern

thought which began with the Enlightenment which, in both its aims and principles, differs fundamentally from the Reformation.

Even those who never read Luther's truly magnificent books about the church "the communion of saints," should recognize that Luther was deeply concerned with the church. In this communion which God himself has established, God's saving work in this world is realized, and it is, therefore, an essentially supernatural order within the finite realm. What the Reformers considered essential in the concept of the church can best be presented in three phases.

Firstly, they were not intent upon destruction of the medieval church or anxious to establish a church of their own. They longed for the restoration of the ancient church, the church of the New Testament.

They were at one with most of their contemporaries when they insisted that a reform was necessary, and that it should go further than the correction of a few particularly glaring abuses. There was general agreement that the reform should be thorough or, in the language of that day, "a reform of head and members." The Evangelicals differed from their contemporaries in their insistence that this reform should go all the way to the beginnings—the church of the New Testament itself. The New Testament became the standard by which they judged what the church ought to be. This accounts unquestionably for the amazing success of the Reformation. The abuses in the visible church had become so numerous, they were so much in the foreground, and appeared so deeply rooted, that nothing less than a determined return to the classical beginnings seemed to offer a satisfactory solution.

When Luther retraced his steps to the beginnings of the Christian church, he did not thereby disregard what history had created in the meantime. Unlike Münzer and other "en-thusiasts," and much later Tolstoi, Luther never wished to disown the history and traditions of the church and make the Sermon on the Mount a literally binding code of law for a restored church. It is well known that Luther treated the traditions of the church gently and with genuine under-standing.

A casual visitor who attended a church service in Witten-berg in the third decade of the sixteenth century would have been aware of only one difference. The words of institu-tion were not mumbled in Latin but spoken audibly in Ger-man; everything else appeared unchanged. In this, as in every other respect, Luther was no revolutionary. His con-cern was always with principles and fundamentals, with the standards of the New Testament itself. His ideal of the true church was derived from the writings of the apostles and evangelists.

This concentration upon essentials determines also the second distinctive element in his doctrine of the church. He had often defined the nature of the true church. His great treatise, "On the Councils and the Churches" (1539), is something like a systematic treatment of the subject and contains quite a few deviations from the official contempo-rary view of the nature of the church. He names as one of the *notae ecclesiae,* the marks of the church, "the possession of the Holy Cross" and points thereby to an aspect of the church that had been almost forgotten amidst the splendor of the medieval church: the true church is always a supressed and persecuted church. He often wrote about the church, either as a subject by itself or in connection with some other topic, but always reached the same conclusion—the distin-guishing mark of the church is the presence of Christ.

Christ is present in the teaching, as far as it is pure and

authentic without human additions and qualifications, centered in him alone. He, who himself is the Word of God (John 1; Rev. 19), manifests himself in the preaching of the church. Where he is proclaimed in faith and received in faith, there, and there alone, is the church. For this reason the doctrine of the real presence of Christ in Word and Sacrament is so essential. A deep gulf separates Luther's understanding of the church from the diluted, psychologizing interpretations of today. A truly higher world is present in the "communion of saints." The church is not the association of "religious people," but the activity of the living God, who calls and works with and blesses the human race which is deeply involved in guilt and death. This view of the church is important for two reasons. It really accepts the church as a divine institution. It is evident that only such a church can count on a future in this world. Every humanized church by its very adaptation to the human situation becomes involved in mankind's most tragic fate, impermanence and mortality. How quickly such a fate can overtake it is best demonstrated by the last great representative of a humanized *ecclesia,* the national church. Though every genuine church belongs to the historical reality of the nation in whose midst it is at work and can never exist in a vacuum, "church" means always God's activity, God's dealing with men. It is therefore always more than just a factor in a nation's history.

Where man attempts to shape the form or, more seriously, the essence of the church in conformity with the course of secular history or national prejudices or cultural needs, he usurps the prerogatives of God. It does not take long, as a rule, until God makes it evident through further developments that he delegates his sovereign rights over the church to no man. The history of the church speaks loudly enough, provided we are ready to listen. That also explains another feature of Lutheranism which is frequently regarded as weakness, yet is nothing of the sort. The Lutheran Church is basically quite indifferent toward all forms of ecclesiastical organization and polity. This peculiarity is so characteristic that one cannot easily overlook it. It distinguishes Lutheranism from Catholicism in a far more fundamental manner than is ordinarily recognized. In the Roman Church the ecclesiastical organization, the institution, is of basic religious significance. The pope is not merely the administrative head of a closely knit organization; to recognize and obey him becomes a prerequisite for salvation, and the same condition applies to the rest of the hierarchy.

Polity has no religious significance in the Lutheran Church. Individual sociologists will find it either amazing or annoying that the Lutheran Church can assume so many forms of historical existence, varying all the way from an officially governed state church with a king as its titular head (as in Scandinavia, and Germany before the first world war) to the independent, democratically organized, flourishing congregations in North America. All of them, however, are Lutheran churches because all of them share one indispensable characteristic, purity in the teaching of the Word and administration of the Sacraments.

The historian may want to know whether the church would not have gained outwardly if a firmer organization had been available in times of crisis. While it is true that certain temporary advantages had to be sacrificed, the church itself remained in a position to preserve its own true genius. Two fundamental principles are joined together in the Lutheran doctrine of the church. The Lutheran church is the church of Jesus Christ, but the church of Christ is not confined to only one communion. The church is wherever Christ is preached and accepted in faith. This attitude enabled Luther to be remarkably forebearing in theory and practice and, thereby, establish a pattern for his church. Just as he never denied that Christ could be found in the papal church even during the worst periods, so would we not withhold recognition from any church which gives room to the gospel. It is of great practical importance that, following Luther's example, the church that bears his name has never invaded the territory of any other church or made attempts to proselyte.

We must testify of Christ; humans can do no more, but must leave the outcome in God's hands. This is a far more magnanimous approach than the mistaken zeal of some sects who sought their converts among the members of the church, instead of reaching out for those who have no faith.

The novelist Novalis, in an essay entitled "Christendom and Europe," once painted an unforgettable portrait of occidental Christendom: the flock of European nations under the guidance of a benevolent shepherd in Rome; under him serve a large group of devoted priests who preserve one faith among these varied peoples.

Our problem is not whether such a state of affairs ever existed in Europe. The fact is that the only future the church can expect in the world is as a church of Christ, where the presence of the Saviour means everything, and problems of external organization are ultimately unimportant.

One of the greatest living Christians in the Eastern church, Mereschkovski, has recently concluded a brilliant analysis of the European church with this observation: "If the church has a way to the future, it is the path of Martin Luther." Luther was deeply concerned with the universality of the church. It is wrong, both systematically and historically, to describe the church of the Reformation as a fragment, a split from the church universal. The opposite is true, the Reformers felt a profound responsibility for the unity of the church. The historical situation has changed, the task has remained. Wherever men know of the church at all, they also yearn for the ecumenicity of that church. Through the ages Christians have confessed their faith in "One Holy and Apostolic Church," but the desire for this unity has never been more intense and vital than today.

How can this unity be realized? The answer of the Reformers is almost classical in its simplicity and discernment: where Christ is preached and accepted in faith, there is the *whole* church. Where Christ is present in the Word which carries his power and his spirit and awakens faith in man, there can be no partial church, representing a partial truth. The whole church must be there. Where communion with Christ becomes a reality, the mission of the church is fulfilled; it has reached the highest status of which it is capable, even as a visible, historical phenomenon. The church can never be an association of self-sufficient individuals. It is always the great host of believers throughout the ages among whom the call to faith occurs. No one ever became a believer except through the ministrations of God's servants and his fellow Christians. Where faith in the living Christ takes root in a human heart, the person enters *ipso facto* into the fellowship of all believers.

We must not look upon the church as an institution that has been subjectively developed in response to the religious needs and aspirations of individuals. The church is always born of the call of Christ which is transmitted by his servants. Only where Christ is preached in faith and faith is thereby awakened, can the church come into being. It never comes as the result of the "search for God" by which natural man reaches out for an object on which he can center his personal religious feelings. Luther was extremely anxious to preserve the church as an objective reality. To describe the church of the Reformation as the church of subjectivism is an unjustifiable, undeserved misrepresentation. Though the error is common, it is by no means always intended as adverse criticism. It does, however, misjudge Luther's own position. In fact, Luther contends that the papal church of his day had succumbed to subjectivism, because it had made such extensive and unwarranted concessions to the elemental religious cravings of man. In the Articles of Schmalkalden, Luther places the Catholic affinity for natural religion alongside the "subjectivism" of the spiritualists and calls both tendencies, somewhat crudely, "enthusiasm." He henceforth connotes by that term man's inherent religious impulse which misleads him into the belief that he can find his way to God by his own initiative and through his own effort.

Luther sensed here a subtle but very real danger. Genuine faith which takes hold of God's revelation (and that means Christ) is never the humanly evolved response to a religious "postulate" but is always created by the "external" Word and Sacrament. It is of utmost importance that such faith should not rest upon our changing human emotions but upon the eternal foundation of that which "God has done for us." Because these are the fundamental laws of God, no ecclesiastical evolution can go beyond them. The true church, therefore, the church in which Christ is present through the faithful preaching of the Word, has always been in existence. To deny such a claim, one would have to make the monstrous assertion that during certain periods of history there was no church. The future of this church is likewise independent of the historical development.

Like all objects of faith it is not relegated to a transcendent future but belongs boldly in the present visible reality. It is, of course, true of the church (as of other objects of faith) that it will never achieve perfect stature in the course of its earthly history. All objects of faith constantly point beyond themselves to a fulfillment in that world of eternity where they originated.

The mere analysis of the fundamental principles which went into the evangelical understanding of the nature of the church will not do full justice to our problem. The Reformation divided Christendom into two confessional branches. Is this division justifiable before the judgment of history? What were its effects upon the further course of events? There can be no question that it bisected the Western world into two confessional camps and that the political, intellectual, and cultural life of the West has been permanently marked by this division. Those unable to discover any other effects of the Reformation can usually wax very eloquent when they discuss the "unfortunate split," a stereotyped phrase which has enjoyed the widest circulation.

These complaints should be rejected for some very weighty reasons. They are usually indicative of a lack of historical perspective. While one can appreciate the position of a devout Catholic who regrets the existence of a schism and desires the return of the "heretic" to the bosom of "Mother Church," there is no reason why others, presumably taking a long-range view, should arrive at the same conclusion. *No one can undo the past.*

It is entirely unprofitable to speculate whether the unification of Italy or Germany in the nineteenth century could have been brought about in a manner different from the one in which it actually occurred. It is equally meaningless to discuss the Reformation as though it had been caused by the recklessness of an individual Augustinian monk who had thereby mischievously destroyed a beautiful, flourishing, spiritual communion.

What actually took place in the Reformation was one of

the great moments of destiny, perhaps the greatest in the Western world since the conflict with the forces of Islam. No nation chooses for itself the time when destiny shall strike. Through long and often painful processes of preparation, a nation is made ready for its hour of decision. If the Lord of history ever becomes manifest, it is at the crossroads of history. No matter how many details are adduced to explain the total event, there remains a mysterious element that defies all attempts at a purely rational interpretation. Why did it happen at this and no other period? What dynamics were released at this point? Who are the men and women who act here and become God's instruments and accomplish God's tasks? Luther fully understood and appreciated these hidden forces which ultimately weave the pattern of history.[1]

It is, therefore, a lack of historical acumen (leaving aside for the moment the understandable Catholic position) to interpret such fateful events on the basis of irrelevant standards which, moreover, were formed under the entirely changed conditions of a later era.

One example will illustrate the harm that can be done by such injudicious reading of history. It has recently become a fad to hold the Reformation responsible for the political disunity of Germany. One may as well blame the obvious social inequalities of German life upon the fact that we are dealing here with an agricultural as well as an industrial nation, and that the rural population clings stubbornly to traditional methods of farming and soil conservation. In other words, a problem that has become acute at the moment is blamed on conditions that have existed for centuries.

No romantic ideas or childish speculations can reverse the trend toward the growing industrialization of life. Much less

---

[1] See Hanns Lilje, *Luther's Geschichtsauffassung (Luther's Concept of History)*, Berlin: Furche-Verlag, 1932.

can such a movement as the history of faith, whose roots reach much deeper and involve much greater mysteries, be simply wished out of existence. It is difficult to believe that such criticisms could ever be voiced in earnest. In the very recent past they were certainly nothing more than propagandistic slogans.[2]

Such views are not even straightforward rationalizations but, like all rationalization, fabricated on the basis of ulterior motives. Men tend to shrink timidly from conflict, and spiritual conflict is no exception—while at the same time they are ready to condone and even glory in the mechanized mass murder of modern warfare. Because the historical necessity for spiritual conflict is no longer understood, there is no longer any understanding of the blessings which flow from such conflicts, in spite of whatever tragedy may be involved.

Europe—and in a narrower sense, Germany—has been the battlefield for the intellectual struggles of history. Man's great spiritual decisions have been reached almost exclusively on European soil ever since Christianity began. That is particu-

---

[2] "Luther, who claimed that he wished to renew the church in the spirit of early Christianity, entered upon the path of heretical separatism. He tore the German spirit from the common heritage of the Christian tradition and led it into isolation and loneliness. St. Boniface with a blow of his hatchet had struck at German religious particularism and created the condition for a unified empire on German soil. Luther with his ninety-five theses laid the axe to the religious roots of the empire and prepared the cultural and spiritual dualism by which the German people were divided in their deepest feelings and convictions." From *Universalism and Federalism*, by F. J. Hylander (Munich, 1946).

This is a fine example of the tendency to see everything as either black or white. Do these historians of the Hitler era realize the weakness of their claim that "religious separation" accounts for Germany's political ineffectiveness? None of the religiously homogeneous nations of Europe remained politically strong, neither Catholic Spain nor the Catholic countries of southern Europe, nor Lutheran Scandinavia. History was made by the nations with a religiously mixed population. The moment of personal decision, which Ranke had stressed, came to the fore and proved the most vital element in shaping the course of history.

larly true of Germany, located between East and West, without natural boundaries and thus predestined, it appears, to be the battleground of Europe. This fact, so rarely understood by other nations, accounts for the tragic character of German history and the brooding temperament of its people. Where else has the anguish of faith plumbed such depths? If we ask for proof, we need only look at the Catholic Church. How different is the piety of the German peasant from that of a southern Italian or Spaniard. The steady encounter with Protestantism in Germany has done the Catholic Church no harm. It has gained by the fact that it was thereby forced into a position of never-ceasing self-examination and vigilance. The experience of the sixteenth century is repeated here. The Council of Trent had codified Catholic doctrine and thereby made the wall between the churches insurmountable. After the doctrinal differences had been pointedly enumerated at Trent, it became even more impossible for Protestants to return to the Church of Rome than it had been before.

But the Roman Church itself had been reawakened and had discovered a new vitality which enabled it once more to function with vigor and effectiveness. Paradoxical as it may seem, the church of the papacy owes its reformation to the impulses which emanated from Martin Luther.

It would be wrong to distrust or belittle the ardent hope for an end of this separation which is often expressed in our day. It is the natural reaction to the serious challenge which the contemporary situation presents to the church. One would not be a true disciple unless one felt the tragedy inherent in this separation and shared the hope which Christ himself expressed: *Ut omnes unum sint.*

No real disciple of Christ, on the other hand, will expect that a change can be wrought by purely human efforts. Attempts of this nature have actually never ceased, and accompany the history of the church as shadow follows light. They prove conclusively that no human endeavor can achieve what God alone can give, be it in time or beyond the realm of time. The fundamental inconsistency in all these negotiations has been classically stated by the French theologian Bossuet, the court chaplain of Louis XIV. During a conference with a Lutheran abbot[3] and a Spanish Franciscan,[4] he remarked: "If your faith is the same as ours, why do you persist in separation? If you feel, however, in good conscience that you have valid reasons for your dissension, how could we possibly reach an agreement?"

Nevertheless, a sense of resignation, a feeling that all efforts are futile, need not and should not have the last word. For never in the course of its long history has Christianity ever been faced with such a fundamental spiritual threat. While in the past heresies were directed against certain aspects of Christianity, or non-Christian forces such as the Arabs reached out for Christian lands, today we face the far more serious threat of the universal rejection of Christianity in its entirety. Yet, at this very moment when the whole earthly future of Christianity has become problematical, there is a new emphasis upon the great convictions, the ultimate views on life which all Christians hold in common: the Christian view of man as opposed to an atomistic, atheistic materialism; Christian ideals of the family and the education of youth in contrast to a corroding nihilism; the whole Christian orientation towards life, death, and eternity. In spite of deep-seated doctrinal differences, there is a united front against a non-Christian world which constitutes a stronger more effective bond than all planned efforts to achieve union at the organizational level. This is a shining demonstration of the reality

---

[3] Gerhard Molanus of Loccum.
[4] Spinola.

of "one holy Christian Church." Like every other great Christian truth, this is not only a hope to be realized but a fact which is already in existence. In this respect Christians have never been more united than they are today.

The question as to what the future holds for the church, particularly the Protestant church, must be sought on this plane. Can it be a simple unbroken continuation of the forms that have come down from the past? Before we can decide, we must determine what Lutheran Protestantism thinks about the nature of the church.

We have already called attention to the flexibility of Lutheran concepts of the church. They include the most rigidly ritualistic state church and the independent, self-governed congregation. All of them however, hold one conviction in common—the supreme concern of the church is always the presence of Christ. Another characteristic mark of the Lutheran Church is the fact that it is always the church of the Bible and the hymnbook. While the church has widely differed in matters of organization and administration, the essence, that which makes it a church, has always remained the same, in spite of the varied forms which its outward appearance has presented. Strangely enough, only one great Lutheran theologian, Martin Kähler (1835-1912) has attempted to write a history which traces the impact of the Bible upon life. One must keep in mind what it meant for former generations and for the church itself that the church of Luther was a Bible-centered and Bible-reading church.

The fact is not always clearly recognized because modern Europeans, the Germans among them, have become completely estranged from biblical knowledge and biblical thinking. All through the nineteenth century British intellectuals retained a much greater familiarity with the Bible than did this same class in Germany. The estrangement started in Germany early in the nineteenth century. Goethe still felt a closeness to the Scriptures which amazes his modern compatriots. When he wished to express his admiration for something fundamental and pure in history, he described it in these words, "One breathes here the pure air of the patriarchs." Before his mind's eye he saw the green virgin soil where the flocks of Abraham grazed and men were still close to God. (He was, of course, unaware how greatly modern historical research had changed this idyllic picture; it would have meant little to him, had he known.) The men and women of Goethe's day could still speak in the majestic language of the Luther Bible, revel in its vivid imagery, and think its timeless truths.

One need not belabor the point that they knew a source of power and richness which has been lost to our metaphysically impoverished, nihilistic age. Familiarity with the Bible has been a potent factor in the shaping of history. Germany's recovery after the Thirty Years' War was not the work of the literati but of Lutheran preachers and heads of families, who knew their Bible and Catechism and, thereby, the divine rules by which the life of a nation could be reconstructed.

Far too few people have ever heard of the "underground" Protestantism in Austria which maintained itself for centuries against the harsh measures of the official Counter Reformation. In little huts, high in the mountains of Carinthia and Salzburg, people read their Bibles behind locked doors and preserved a Lutheran church of such vitality that it surprised everybody when this Protestant church emerged into the light, after Emperor Joseph II had issued his decrees of toleration.

Little needs to be said about the Lutheran hymnal. The chorale is the most characteristic creation of Lutheran Protestantism. At a time when the Jesuits expressed their genius artistically in the charming, and always slightly theatrical,

141

baroque style, Protestantism became articulate in the cantatas and passions of Bach. At Bach's hands the chorale received its most mature treatment, and in the most spiritual of all arts it reached a perfection that has never been surpassed.

It is remarkable how timeless the quality of this music is, and how great its power to move men of our generation by its undimmed freshness and originality. The discerning among our contemporaries realize that one cannot maintain it, if it is uprooted from the soil in which it has matured.

This great music has been a source of strength and comfort to countless people because faith has inspired it and the glory of eternity vibrates in it. Through the centuries the Lutheran hymnbook has gladdened the hearts of worshipers, for its hymns are not forms of lyric expressions of the religious feelings of individuals, but documents of the experiences of generations who have sung and confessed and prayed these words.

The catechism should also be mentioned in this connection. Its influence upon the development of the German language has already been pointed out. Its importance can be determined by the fact that it was the first Lutheran innovation which was adopted by the Catholic Church for its own use. The *Catechismus Romanus* was compiled at Trent. The Roman Church has thereby shown a greater appreciation of this teaching aid than the educators of a later, more sentimental age who complained bitterly about medievalism and mechanical memorization. There is a great difference between a generation that has acquired a knowledge of basic Christian truths and learned to think in its terms, and a generation for whom the world of religion is *terra incognita,* and which is, therefore, completely agnostic with regard to ultimate issues. Today everyone can see for himself how great this difference really is.

This whole discussion, though necessary in order to establish facts, is limited in its scope. Bible and hymnbook, catechism and chorale have been the marks of Lutheranism in an era that has now come to an end. It is the fate of everything human to be subject to distortion. Protestantism, though it attempted to remain faithful to its principles, is no exception to the rule. All the great churches have, in the process of pursuing their own characteristic genius, become open to secularization. The Catholic Church tends towards secularization in the sphere of political activity, the Calvinistic churches in their preoccupation with problems of social justice, and a misguided Lutheranism in its stress on the pseudo-scientific— the theoretical. For whole generations the outstanding weakness of Lutheranism has been the intellectualization of the faith. The Danish critic Kierkegaard warned repeatedly that Protestantism would thereby become the religion of a self-satisfied middle class, a danger which has constantly become more real since the middle of the last century. It is a serious menace, indeed, but like all other threats to the life of the church it cannot be overcome by passing resolutions or adopting programs of activity. As a matter of fact, help has come from somewhere else. Since the Lord of history has already crushed the last remains of a bourgeois civilization in Europe, the church has been set free from many premises which were once thought indispensable. They are now recognized for what they were, mere scaffolding which the church does not need in order to be a church.

At the moment it is impossible to discern in detail what forms the life of the church will assume in the future. One fact is certain—it can never be a return to previously held positions. The church cannot prove her loyalty to the work of Martin Luther by standing still, either in the sixteenth or the nineteenth century. She must advance in faith and obedience upon the road that has once been pointed out to her.

It may mean the sacrifice of many historical institutions

which she has treasured and found useful in dealing with the public. Her heritage of cultural accomplishments will pale with that culture itself. The church, however, is not destined to die like all human creations which are subject to vanity.

The church of tomorrow, in all her branches, will resemble the church of the first centuries much more than the church of the liberal era ever could. The Lutheran Church has the least reason to fear these changes, for she has never attached undue importance to institutional or organizational structure. She will take her Bible, the Word of God, into the coming era, she will sing her hymns in a new age. The Commandments, the Lord's Prayer, the confessions of faith will be the same amidst the changing conditions of life.

The new experiences she will need—the firmer faith in a world beyond, the readiness to sacrifice and suffer, a more fervent charity—will not come as results of better human planning. They will come as divine gifts from God's hands, in answer to the church's prayers.

The Foundations of
the Modern Era

The Reformation assumed such far-reaching importance in history because it occurred at the beginning of the so-called modern era. What that means in detail and where we must look for the effects of the Reformation have become largely obscured. That is understandable. So many "new eras" have appeared since Luther's time[1] that most contemporaries find it difficult to think of the past four centuries as a continuity with which we still maintain a vital and meaningful relationship.

It is so, nevertheless. A historical process is never brought to an abrupt end, and the European civilization of today is, in many of its fundamental aspects, the outcome of the Reformation, no matter how greatly these aspects have changed in the meantime. We have already shown what the Reformation has done in the more immediate areas of faith and church life. We must now demonstrate its effects upon political, intellectual, and cultural life.

What were the forces which eventually consolidated Protestantism into a political and historical entity? The question leads to one of the most complicated, and in many respects

---

[1] It was one of the tenets of National Socialism in Germany that the movement represented a decisive break with the past and opened a new era in history. (Tr.)

most disappointing, chapters in the history of the Reformation. At this point the development of Lutheranism compares very unfavorably with that of the other branches of Protestantism. A brief glance will make that clear.

We can disregard the political radicalism of the "enthusiasts." It did not need the tragic collapse of the peasant rebellion of 1525 or the brutal, bloody foolishness of the Anabaptists at Münster in 1534 to prove that absolute radicalism always fails in the end. Not even Mohammed or Genghis Khan or Napoleon could defy this law of history. There were, however, men among the Reformers who knew how to conduct themselves with firmness in the political arena and plan with vision and determination. The political urge of the Reformation is far more strongly expressed in them than in Luther. Zwingli is unquestionably the most important among them. We have learned to appreciate him and his ideals much better since his writings have become available. We obviously do him an injustice if we dispose of him as a mere rationalistic humanist. The humanistic style in which he presents his evangelical convictions is like "a garment that has become too small." It is, however, his exceptional ability and his strong will to political action which mark him as the politically outstanding figure among the Protestant theologians. He tried to establish a theocratic government and did it far more resolutely and consistently than Calvin in Geneva. He strove ably and unselfishly for a united Protestantism. His death in battle, which took many hopeful beginnings to the grave with him, is as apt a symbol as we have of the Reformation. He alone of the great Reformers offered up his life while yet young for the sake of his convictions—and he did not fall as a combatant but as a chaplain, though for political and military reasons he had advised against the campaign and disapproved of it. It was only natural that his keen political instinct felt an immediate affinity for that other great political leader among the Protestants, Philip of Hesse. The famous debate at Marburg in 1529 was bound to fail. Zwingli and Philip were anxious to devise a formula which would enable the Protestants to co-operate in political matters, though they held divergent views on the doctrine of the Lord's Supper. They moved on an altogether different plane from Luther, for whom biblical clarity and truth meant much more than political opportunities.

Calvin follows Zwingli in this area only at a considerable distance. He was more an administrator than a political thinker, more rigid in his planning and without that flexibility which is so important for any true statesman. He did not equal Zwingli either in character or ability. It is interesting that Calvin always spoke of Luther with great respect and personal warmth, though the Reformer of Wittenberg had treated him rather rudely. His opinion of Zwingli, on the other hand, was unfavorable, even acrimonious. He felt the difference, probably sensed that Zwingli possessed exactly those qualities which he lacked. Calvin, unlike Luther, entered directly into the field of practical politics. He did not hesitate to give concrete political advice to rulers, for instance Princess Margaret of Navarre; and he participated energetically in such purely secular affairs as the negotiations of an alliance between Geneva and Berne. Such activities were utterly foreign to Luther's nature. Calvin's most significant political achievement was the organization of the Protestant church in France. So well did he do his work that he made it possible for the Huguenots to take their heroic stand upon the foundations which he laid. He is indirectly responsible for the world-wide outlook of Anglo-Saxon Protestantism. The Church of Scotland and the Puritans of the new world owe their church life to the impetus of John Calvin. He is, indeed, a figure of world-wide importance.

When we think of one of the great Catholic leaders of that day, Ignatius Loyola, who did not confine his spiritual strategy to the royal courts of Europe but encompassed the Far East in his globe-circling vision, Luther the *politician* becomes dwarfed. Such sweeping ambitions were unknown in Wittenberg. It is true that students from every country of Europe swarmed into the little Saxon university town and carried the new faith to the Scandinavian countries in the North and the newly emerging national states of eastern Europe. Important as the changes were which these messengers of a reformed gospel finally effected, they can hardly be termed political changes in the strict sense of the word.

It is almost unbelievable that Luther, with his keen sense for history, could practice political reticence to the point where it actually endangered the course of Protestantism. He saw world events clearly enough to speak out fearlessly on world politics and the Turkish menace; he found his way intuitively through the political intrigues at Worms; he addressed princes with a candor bordering on rudeness; he rarely erred in his opinions of princes and diets; and, unlike Melanchthon, he had no political illusions. But he had none of Zwingli's political talent and passion and therefore none of his political ambitions. The historian can readily point to favorable political opportunities which he ignored, and others in which he actually harmed the cause of Protestantism by his refusal to take its political future into consideration. He really symbolizes in his person the political renunciation of Lutheranism which so often became evident in the course of world events.

Two factors should in fairness be considered. One of them is the psychological. Luther's aversion to political activity is the self-limitation of the genius. Like all extremely gifted individuals he had a variety of talents. He was a theologian, musician, linguist, and administrator. When he shunned the actual business of politics, he demonstrated his ability to stay within his limitations. Goethe showed similar discernment in the distinction between elements which he found congenial and others which were foreign to his temperament.[2]

The other factor is more important in the long run. When Luther relinquished his opportunity to decide the political configuration of the Reformation and confined himself to "principles," he actually preserved the Reformation. He made it possible for the church to exist under varying forms of government and to be independent of changes in the political sphere.

The opposite is frequently claimed. It is said that Luther delivered the Reformation into the hands of secular powers, "betrayed it to the princes." Some scholars have even gone so far as to assert that the real core of the Reformation is a radical reversal of authority. Heretofore questions of faith and piety had always been decided by the spiritual powers; Luther had turned them over to the state.[3] The average European is fully convinced that Luther is responsible for the fateful combination which is characterized by the phrase "throne and altar."

But this conclusion misrepresents the facts. It is, of course, true that Luther had solicited help from the princes when the time came to complete the work of the Reformation in the legal and political sphere. During Luther's own lifetime,

---

[2] Goethe once declared that one must never leave the fortifications of one's own particular temperament.

[3] That is hardly correct and in any event the process was not confined to Lutheran territories. A national church with a secular ruler as its head existed in the Calvinistic countries of Switzerland, Holland, Scotland. The Anglican "Reformation" of the sixteenth century consisted solely in this change. One finally finds the same situation in the Catholic nations of France and Spain.

particularly during the last decade, the political leadership of the Reformation had already passed into the control of the territorial princes.

This transfer of authority, however, was meant as a temporary measure, because there was no one else to assume this responsibility, and the emergency nature of the arrangement was generally understood during the formative years of the Reformation. It must be admitted in fairness that the princes performed the task that had been thrust upon them as well as conditions permitted. That it should fall to their lot was inevitable. Only under one condition could it have been avoided. The church would have had to renounce its right to be a public body within the public realm and establish itself as a private society. Such an alternative simply did not exist at that time. Private associations for the cultivation of the religious life did not make their appearance in Europe until the eighteenth century. Even such radical Reformers as Thomas Münzer and his peasants, who attempted to put their extreme political views into practice in the mock government of Münster, still show that the struggle for church and organized Christianity was always a struggle for public and legal recognition.

Because the emperor was personally opposed to the Reformation and all its ideals, he eliminated himself from leadership. It was left to the princes to act in the public realm. Let us restate the facts: Even where the princes failed, they performed their task as well as the circumstances permitted. Speculations, avarice, vainglory, and political ambitions may have played a part in their administration, yet the responsibility was theirs. Luther made no mistake when he called upon the princes for assistance. It merely proved his realistic recognition of that which was historically possible. We shall notice that he constantly impressed upon the princes the sacredness of this trust and reminded them of obligations far greater than the satisfaction of personal greed and vanity. He never claimed that the call of the princes grew out of any principle. His clear distinction between the two realms of state and church counteracted any harm that may have arisen from the temporary fusion of the two and constitutes Luther's permanent contribution toward the solution of the problem. The Lutheran Church is not committed to any particular form of political organization. It is not necessarily a state church or a free church. There is a place for these and similar terms, provided they are not meant to establish a principle. The church is where Christ is preached and accepted in faith, be it a state church or a free association, a national church or a church based on voluntary membership. The historical variety of forms the Lutheran Church has taken bears that out. In Scandinavia it is state church, rich in liturgical traditions, endowed with the legal prerogatives of a church that has for centuries been identified with the life of the population. We find it as a purely voluntary organization with all the external marks of a democracy in the Anglo-Saxon world, flourishing particularly in the United States. Since 1918 the Lutheran Church of Germany occupies a position somewhere between these. It is neither a state church nor a private association, but a public institution. History thus furnishes the illustrations for the already mentioned principle, that the essence of the church is independent of its political structure.

Before we explore this further we must briefly survey the events which brought the political evolution of the Reformation to a close. The bearers of this evolution were, as already stated, the princes. Notwithstanding Luther's personal aversion to political action, the Reformation counted among its adherents some highly gifted political leaders. They, with the assistance of able jurists and upright statesmen, raised all the questions during the decisive years. Among the Catholic princes none was their equal. The really outstanding antagonist was the emperor himself. Planning carefully, stubborn to the point of obstinacy, cautious to the point of procrastination, he pursued one goal throughout his life, the restoration of religious unity.

It is one of the tragedies of history that this contest did not yield a clear-cut decision. The emperor who was wholly sincere in his motives, spent his last years in resignation. Successful in many of his undertakings, he had failed in the one which had been the supreme ambition of his life. The Protestant cause suffered an irreparable setback at the moment of its greatest opportunity through the tragic weakness of its ablest champion, the Elector of Hesse.

The German princes have played a deplorable, occasionally even unsavory, role throughout the course of German history. Luther often referred to them as "poor, benighted fools with whom God has undoubtedly afflicted us in his great wrath." Nevertheless, as leaders of the Reformation they did their part, and at certain periods, notably around 1550, they did it better than the theologians. It was their determined stand which made possible Luther's appearance at Worms. They insisted on presenting their protests at Speyer and acquired thereby the name Protestants. Though repeated attempts such as the meeting at Marburg failed to unify Protestantism, they had enough vision to create a system of alliances which was a real danger to their opponents. It came to be known as the League of Schmalkalden, named after the sleepy little town of Schmalkalden in Thuringia. The league was vexed by internal tensions, rivalries, and indecision, but it was so superior to its counterpart, the Catholic League under the personal leadership of the emperor, that it could impose its will upon its antagonists.

It was therefore particularly unfortunate that, at the most critical moment, the force of the movement was lost through the personal fault of Philip of Hesse. The blow came as an aftermath to the matrimonial difficulties of the margrave. He had fallen in love with the sister of his wife's lady-in-waiting, the Baroness Margarete von der Saale. The young lady, or rather her mother, declined to agree to an illicit relationship, an established custom at European courts, and insisted upon legal marriage. Philip's wife refused to surrender her rights and the only way out of the impasse seemed to be a polygamous marriage. The Reformers, partially misinformed by the prince, finally gave the "confessional counsel" to enter into a double marriage. In giving such advice, they took the margrave's "conflict of conscience" into consideration, and based their instruction upon the Old Testament practice of the patriarchs who were simultaneously married to several wives.

The Reformers made it a condition to keep this whole matter secret. It is difficult to understand why they ever gave such advice or expected that knowledge of this affair could be withheld from the public. Philip's conduct was not only offensive to Christian morality but in violation of the secular laws against bigamy. Apart from every other consideration, the legal offense had compromised Philip with the emperor. The latter made clever use of the margrave's predicament. He let it be known that Philip could count on leniency if he would listen to reason in the matter of Protestant leadership. As a result, Protestantism lost its most resourceful adviser at a time when he was urgently needed. The Electors of Saxony continued the fight with ability and courage, but Charles had gained his aim. The Protestant forces tired of the struggle and withdrew to more favorable military positions in southern Germany. Charles followed them and won the brilliant victory at Mühlberg in 1547. The Protestants were almost annihilated. It was Charles's most important and glorious military achievement. Titian's portrait has preserved this moment of Charles's greatest military and political triumph. It shows the emperor in glittering armor as he proudly rides across the battlefield.

The two leaders of the Protestant army, the Landgrave of Hesse and the Elector of Saxony, had become his prisoners. Protestantism appeared doomed, but by his chronic indecision the emperor lost all the advantages he had gained. A character trait which had often saved him in critical situations now became his undoing. He did not exploit his victory, and the Protestants under the energetic young Elector Moritz of Saxony had time to reorganize their forces. They struck with such lightening suddenness that the emperor was barely able to escape from Innsbruck. The situation was once more reversed and more in keeping with the actual state of affairs of which the peace treaty of 1555, which provided religious equality, was little more than an outward acknowledgement.

The great conflict did not lead to a clear decision. The real importance of the treaty lies in the fact that religious toleration was for the first time recognized in Europe, at least in the imperial cities.

Protestantism had not gained the undisputed leadership which for decades appeared to be within its reach, but it had survived. The imperial policy fell even more drastically short of its aims. It failed to achieve the most ambitious of its world-wide undertakings, the restoration of religious unity in Europe.

It is indicative of the depth and tragedy of this struggle that it had to continue for another century. The treaty of Westphalia, which concluded it in 1648, was only signed after both parties were utterly exhausted. This whole period of bloodshed and cruelty constitutes one of the blackest chapters in the history of Christianity. The Counter Reformation was besmirched not only by the horrid outrages of the Massacre of St. Bartholomew (August 23, 24, 1572), but was tainted by a long series of equally barbarous but less familiar acts of physical violence and mental torture. The two men who finally terminated the conflict were the two outstanding political leaders of that period, Richelieu and Gustavus Adolphus. In some respects it might even be said that the French cardinal saved German Protestantism—not only on the grounds of French politics but because he somehow recognized the inevitability of all that had happened. Alongside this brilliant diplomat stands the figure of the most outstanding statesman and military leader in the Protestant ranks, the Lutheran king of Sweden. He appeared like a meteor on the horizon and for a brief moment seemed to reach out for the German imperial crown and the realization of the dream of a united Protestant Germany.

When the peace of Westphalia finally put an end to the horrors of thirty years of warfare, the fate that had ruled over Germany became the fate of Europe. Henceforth there were two types of churches in the Christian world. European history was changed by the co-existence of these two communions, and even more by the new faith itself. Protestantism was destined to become not only the strongest but the most important factor in European history. Faith and the church were the fundamental concerns of the Reformation, but this concern reached so deeply into the soil of history that no phase of the so-called modern era remained untouched by it. One encounters, of course, wide differences of opinion when one attempts to determine precisely which factors in modern life owe their existence to the impetus which came originally from the Reformation.

We wish at this point to call attention to three essential

philosophical orientations which are deeply embedded in the structure of modern society. These are concerned with 1) the individual (person-centered thinking), 2) the state, and 3) the intellect.

To think of man as a person has recently been decried as an outmoded form of individualism. It was said to belong to an age we had left behind. The fact is, however, that the problem of man is more vital and relevant today than it has been for a long time. It is impossible to eradicate a yearning, so deep and sincere as the hope for a true humanity, by simply rejecting the quest. Individualism itself was a form of degeneration, but the way to cure an illness is not to destroy the body in which the ailment occurs. It is one of the most ominous indications of our spiritual decline that the opposition to an exaggerated individualism manifests itself now in the disinclination to inquire seriously into the nature of man. The quest itself is lost in the great variety of nihilistic mass movements of every type and description. A generation which can so readily betray the ideal of man's dignity that it no longer even cares to ask for it, is sick unto death and must succumb unless it can overcome its own inertia.

We cannot live in this world unless we know precisely what we mean by humanity. It is not difficult to discard the supercilious concept of the individual which was in vogue until now. A radical individualism which acknowledges nothing beyond Self, which absolutizes its own thoughts and behavior, is obviously an element of negation and must disintegrate as soon as it comes in contact with the most elementary forms of social life. This diversion and all its resultant mischief is so evident that it requires no formal indictment. If we go back, however, beyond the point where this process of disintegration first began, we shall discover that Protestantism had offered the most vital and vigorous view of man evolved in Western thought. It was able to do it because its understanding of man rested upon its understanding of faith. It has been previously stated what faith meant for Luther. Man stands before God in complete loneliness and charged with responsibility. When he appears before God at the moment of death, he has no one who will take his place. Life is likewise an existence which allows of no substitution.[4] God has called us into existence and this call of God alone makes human existence complete. It is therefore uniquely personal and responsible existence. At no other point in Western history has man been taken so seriously. Only where man is recognized as a person can life be a genuine good, and personality can only be achieved by one who has learned to stand in the presence of God.

This position must be guarded against three possible misinterpretations.

1) It is historically wrong to hold Lutheranism responsible for modern "individualism." Every student of history knows that individualism belongs to a later era and appears at its earliest in the writings of Descartes—if one insists on assigning a traffic policeman to the intersection of intellectual avenues. Wherever an error arises, there must have been a truth first, and none but great truths can be distorted into errors. It is not asking too much to insist on a clear differeniation between the great truth of personal existence and its later misinterpretations.

2) It is unfair of Catholic theologians to give the impression that Luther made faith dependent upon a subjective, even subjectivistic premise.[5] Catholic (i.e. Christian) scholars

---

[4] Carlyle found a good phrase for it when he said of the young Cromwell that he lived "ever in his great Taskmaster's eye."

[5] Christopher Dawson, whom I otherwise esteem very highly, habitually refers to Protestant piety as "rational-emotional."

should know better. Luther did not offer a new anthropology, but reiterated the biblical view of man, as prophets and psalmists, apostles and evangelists have proclaimed it. Do these Catholic theologians really care to imply that personal faith was unknown before Luther? How could one explain the great religious thinkers of the early Middle Ages or the expansion of Christianity during the first three centuries, if one denounces personal faith as a form of subjectivism which Luther had introduced into the Christian faith? Were personal conversions, of which the individual was quite cognizant, unknown before the Reformation?

3) Luther did not relegate the individual to a vacuum and isolate him from every other contact. Man becomes truly human precisely for the reason that he stands in relationship to God, derives his existence from him, and remains oriented toward him. One readily perceives the difference between Luther's concept of personality and that of the German philosopher Fichte. Luther's ego is a controlled ego, bound to God and his eternal-temporal order. Fichte upholds the allegedly free ego which is free of every restricting limitation. In view of all that has happened in the world since Fichte philosophized one hundred and thirty years ago, one may rightfully describe his soaring speculations as illusions.

The ingenious systems of German idealism could not provide a philosophical foundation for the rapidly rising technological civilization. (The first attempts at a philosophy of technology bear the stamp of Marxism and materialism.) German idealism proved wholly incapable of preventing the greatest spiritual calamity of our times, the phenomenon of mass mentality (*die Vermassung*). The sociological change from men into masses came as a result of the industrial revolution. Philosophically and spiritually the transformation represents a violent reaction against the ego-speculations of the idealists who permitted personality to be swallowed up in pure abstraction. Luther's ego, on the other hand, is a responsible ego. It is, of course, true that the German philosophers spoke eloquently of the need for personal responsibility, "the moral law within me." A responsibility, however, by which I am in the last analysis responsible to no one but myself is a tautology and ultimately meaningless. A person who is responsible to himself alone is, in the end, not responsible to anyone—that is to say, not responsible at all.

For Luther, faith is never subjectivistic even though it is a personal faith. It does not arise within me but is created by the "external" Word that is brought to me from without. In the same manner, human responsibility is not conceived as subjectivistic by the Reformers but arises as the result of man's encounter with God. This will of God challenges our sense of responsibility. It confronts us in the divine institutions on earth: the natural order (marriage and family); the social order (state, law, education); the soteriological order (church and congregation).

The idealistic concept that every human being starts afresh on the basis of his own premises and insights is pure doctrinairism. It is unrealistic because it ignores the fact that the only life we have is life that is given to us. As truly as we receive physical birth through our parents, our mental life is formed by realities which existed before us. The language in which an individual communicates his ideas was developed by generations that preceded him. The idea patterns in which he is able to think, the nation within whose bounds and destinies he spends his life, are part of the existence that is given to him.

It is expressive of the living character of these divine institutions that they always confront us as persons: father, mother, child, magistrate, preacher, fellow-believer. Throughout the give-and-take relationships of actual life, I do not move in a realm of abstractions, but in contact with real people who become for me the instrumentalities and interpreters of the divine will. Elements which were artificially severed in the bloodless systems of idealism and socialism are conceived here as a harmonious whole. These comments will indicate the principles to which we must return if we wish to find new strength and content for our lives. This is by no means a simple about-face. Quite obviously we cannot act as though we were suddenly back in the sixteenth century. If one has lost one's way, however, it is not necessary to retrace one's course step by step. One can also try to move forward in the right direction until one finally comes out on the right road. Such must be our procedure today. A deliberate return to the past is always an artificial undertaking, and attempts of that sort are nothing but futile and ineffective, romantic gestures. What we can do is to learn to believe and to live here where history has placed us. In fact, we must learn it if our generation is to have any future at all.

This leads to a discussion of Luther's view of the state. His interpretation of the nature of man and the state forms an organic entity.

Burckhardt saw in the great power states "the most significant product of modern history," and these powerful monsters have actually determined the destiny of modern man more than any other single factor. Political loyalty means for the man of the twentieth century what confessional decision meant for the generations of the sixteenth century and the appeal to reason for the men of the eighteenth century. Modern political institutions demand a measure of devotion that was once reserved for religious convictions. They make a claim to absolute truth that formerly belonged to religious dogma. Political intolerance has reached a degree of intensity that was unthinkable in the nineteenth century. For millions of men the political choice has become the most far-reaching, most ultimate, and personal decision of their lives.

It is important therefore to inquire whether a causal relationship exists between the Reformation and the rise of the modern power state. We ask, further, whether the Protestant view of the state is still relevant to our situation today.

A popular theory has it that Luther's chief contribution to political theory is the creation of the "subject mentality." The meaning of the term is well understood: complete acquiescence in public affairs to the point where an individual, in case of necessity, will suppress the voice of his own conscience; full submission to the authority of the state and its ruler as semidivine institutions; the concept of obeying orders as the greatest happiness of a citizen.

The best illustration of such a state is the Hohenzollern monarchy in Germany during the second half of the nineteenth century and its revealing slogan of "throne and altar." The meaning is unmistakable. The church was to confer religious sanction upon a political system whose chief representative was the monarch himself.

Of course, that is not Luther's ideal. This theology of the "underling mentality" presupposes the existence of the omnipotent state which was altogether unknown in the sixteenth century. It did not even originate in a Protestant country but in Catholic France under Louis XIV. He first advanced the political absolutism of state and ruler, elevated the person of the king to a mystical being, and created a palace ritual that was little less than a political liturgy. It is a very serious and almost metaphysical question why this absolutism, after its recession in the nineteenth century, reappeared in the twentieth century in a more accentuated and vicious form than ever before.

We cannot answer the question at the moment. Suffice it to say that the political ideology of the Reformation is of a vastly different character. The imposing ritual at Versailles, the adulation of the king and his regime, are unthinkable at the court of Gustavus Adolphus, though he was also a very able and ambitious king who entertained vast and pretentious projects. It would have been equally impossible at the court of any other Protestant sovereign.

It is essentially the same principle we have already noticed in the concept of man himself. Just as the person is not an absolute Self at the center of the universe who evolves his spiritual ego from within, so the ruler and his government are not the fountainheads of political life but links in the divine order. Luther follows closely the reasoning of St. Paul in Romans 13:2 that every genuine authority on earth is of divine origin or it would not exist at all. This divine character of government was stated by Luther (the "unpolitical" Luther) with such vigor and emphasis that one must concur with his own judgment. No other teacher of Christendom has written as beautifully and usefully about it since the days of the apostles.

Two facts stand out. If the state like every true authority (courts, schools, parents) is of divine origin, it is like every other agency that has its source in God. It is his gift to mankind, his greatest gift as far as the social life of man is concerned. It is protection against chaos. A nation must collapse and disintegrate at the moment the divinely instituted authority ceases to restrain evil. God himself, the Creator of life, does not wish to see human life sink into chaos, where the globe could no longer be the home of mankind. God wants to preserve life on earth, the life of all nations regardless of their belief in him. God who "maketh his sun to rise on the evil and on the good, and sendeth rain on the just and unjust" (Matt. 5:45) desires that all men should benefit from the divine gift of political institutions because historical existence without a national life is impossible. (The Jews are the only significant exception, thereby pointing to a profound mystery in God's plan of history.) Government is "God's minister" (Rom. 13:3-4), its executives are God's "liturgists" (Rom. 13:6).

The political order bears divine dignity. Neither the Scriptures nor the Reformers are particularly concerned with the actual form of this government, and it is a mistake to represent Luther as an obdurate defender of the existing order. As such he would have hardly spoken of "the miserable benighted princes" and warned that one should not follow such "fools" in the wars against the Turks, because the Turks "are ten times more clever and pious than our princes." He reminds rulers who are apt to forget it that they are only humans; from the emperor down they are "poor mortal bags of maggots." He calls them "raving, idiotic, senseless, maniacal, crazy fools."

Expressions like these run through his writings like rushing currents. To call Luther a "servile tool of the princes" is a preposterous catch phrase with no more justification than most slogans. They make it abundantly clear that Luther had no interest in the mystical elevation of the person of the ruler but in the divine institution of orderly government.

A nation, unlike a voluntary association, does not rest upon a contractual agreement between the citizens, in other words upon a voluntary act (one cannot conceive the idea of "resigning" from one's nation) but upon a divinely instituted order.[6] The government does not act in the capacity of

---

[6] The American reader will recognize the running comment against the political philosophy of John Locke. The naturalization laws of every country recognize the right to "resign" one's native citizenship and acquire citizenship in another nation. (Tr.)

a business manager but with authority. The most tangible demonstration of this authority is the fact that the state is the source and guarantor of the judicial process. Anarchy and despotism are forms of degeneration. Both contempt of the state and tyranny are equally impossible for the Christian. The authority of the state is always limited by its double responsibility toward God and man. One need not elaborate the difference between Louis XIV.'s *"L'état c'est moi"* and Luther's concept of government as the servant of God. Through two centuries of Western history there have been repeated attempts to revive the political philosophy of the French monarch, and in two recent instances these possibilities have been carried to their ultimate and horrible extremes.

The growing deification of the state is at the moment the theme of the political history of the West. It is apparently the unavoidable counterpart of the loss of individuality through industrialization, and evidently destined to increase the dehumanization of man. There seems no retreat from this fate unless the Western world returns to the biblical-Reformation insight of the divine nature of the state which imposes obligations upon rulers and subjects, leaders and people alike.

As the human judge must remember that he will have to account for his decisions before the bar of the heavenly Judge, the earthly king needs ever to be mindful that he holds his office as a trust from the King of kings. Only in that way can he hope to escape the dreadful temptation to use his powers arbitrarily. Subjectivistic despotism is the end of political and judicial order. The history of the West during the last two centuries proves conclusively that personal tyranny by a ruler destroys the state.

Rulers experience their responsibility concretely in the relationship with their own subjects. One can match the expression "the divine right of kings" (which came into use in England during the latter part of the seventeenth century) with the term "the divine right of subjects," provided one does not interpret it in the sense of a later parliamentarianism. Obedience is indeed the supreme duty of the citizen. We stress once more that we are speaking of obedience to the divine institution of political order itself. That attitude differs fundamentally from the subservience, servility, and lack of convictions which flourish in subjectivistic civilization and have increased rather than diminished within the recent past.[7] It is evident once more how virile Luther's thinking really was. Only free men are capable of obedience. The slave takes orders, the free man serves out of conviction. Luther frequently referred to the great statement by St. Paul that, in a Christian, obedience is not engendered by force but conviction (Rom. 13:5 "for conscience sake").

In a state which has become absolutized to the point of idol worship, the obedience of free men becomes impossible. Fear of men and contempt for men exist side by side in a totalitarian society—fear of those above, contempt for those below. Christianity demands that we should neither fear nor despise other human beings. That represents precisely the political position of the Reformers.

The obedience of which they speak is genuine obedience; it is not obedience to an individual or a group. The government is not in the same category as an agent who has been instructed to undertake certain social and economic tasks. The government is authority and power. While Luther was always critical of the person of the emperor, he never questioned his right to lead the Germans in the war against the Turks. That function belonged to his imperial office and he could

---

[7] This process had already gone so far in Bismarck's time that he complained about the lack of "civic courage" among the civil servants.

demand obedience for this task. A Christian understands the meaning of true obedience. The Reformers never left any doubt that civic loyalties are ethically determined and differ therefore from simple and unconditional compliance. Blind obedience is un-Christian. Only if one takes the limitations which Luther placed upon civic obedience into consideration can one appreciate the dignity and earnestness of the Protestant position. The limit is reached when loyalty towards the state demands disregard for the commandments of God. The Reformers have demonstrated by their own example that in case of conflict between the commands of the state and the eternal demands of God, Christians may rightfully resist their government. The statements of the Reformers are just as clear as their personal conduct in the matter. The political orientation of the nineteenth century, which gravitated periodically between romanticism and liberalism, has obscured Reformation thinking on this point. In this area we can observe broad and characteristic differences between the leaders. Calvin recognized the right to armed resistance if conscience dictated such a course, and the history of Calvinism furnishes us with the examples of the Huguenots and, to a lesser degree, the career of Cromwell. Calvin approached very closely to the questionable Jesuit counsel that even the assassination of a tyrant is permissible, if no other solution appears in sight. Luther always staunchly maintained that the Christian must refrain from physical violence. His must be the protest of a free man who is bound in his conscience by God and God's order. It is the special task of the church to be the conscience of the rulers and this task she must discharge at all times, without fear or regard of consequences. If this witness goes unheeded, there is nothing left but the silent, poignant testimony of martyrdom. The differences between Calvin and Luther are by no means trivial and have actually prompted different types of conduct in concrete historical situations. But on one decisive issue the Reformers are in complete agreement. Their understanding of civic duty is a far cry from abject and unprincipled submissiveness.

One can easily trace the effects of the Protestant viewpoint through the course of history. The Lutheran prince of the seventeenth century was truly the "father" of his little domain, who had the welfare of his "children" at heart. The achievements of these petty rulers within their domains far surpass in ethical values the exploits of the great totalitarian powers. The latter may rise to great heights of military and economic power, but they have always found it necessary to suppress the consciences of their own nationals. If the great powers are really the most characteristic creation of modern history, the political morality of the Reformers becomes their greatest historical contribution to this generation. Nothing can possibly extricate us from an otherwise insoluble dilemma; we must find our way back to the road we have left.

No other area of life has been as profoundly affected by the Reformation as the broad expanse of general culture. Nowhere else are the ramifications as intricate and the nature of this influence as diversified. Many of these phases of culture have meanwhile become self-sufficient, so that their original relationship to the great religious movement of the sixteenth century is no longer obvious.

It is surprising that this facet of the Reformation is almost universally recognized and acknowledged. No testimony to the Reformation is more wholeheartedly offered than the praise that it "liberated the spirit"—a compliment which is probably undeserved. It rests upon a misunderstanding that arose in the nineteenth century. The Enlightenment saw the great merit of the Reformation in the liberation of the mind, the conscience, and in the new freedom for science.

No one denies that freedom of spirit and conscience, science, and research are positive and precious values which somehow underlie all modern civilization. It would, however, endanger any genuine understanding of the Reformation if we were to minimize the great difference between the ideals of the Reformation and the modern age. We perceive this difference in particularly sharp focus when we examine the tenet "freedom of scientific inquiry" which forms the foundation of all modern science. If one likes to trace the history of ideas, one soon realizes (and it is a sobering realization) that in this respect the Reformation is medieval rather than modern. Though the Reformers released learning from ecclesiastical supervision and used the budding critical scholarship on behalf of their cause, their own scientific temper is much more in harmony with the medieval than with the present outlook. One premise which has completely disappeared from present-day methodology was as firmly held by the Reformers as their scholastic opponents: all scholarship is related to the supernatural. The Reformation gave the scholar independence from the hierarchy for his studies, but it never intended to release scholarship from its ties to God and the God-given order.

The "detached" mentality of our modern era is, from the standpoint of the Reformation, a secularized mentality, an emancipation which has become a despiritualization. This mentality is wholly alien to the temper of the Reformation. Despiritualization is perhaps the most questionable aspect of modern "progress." Jacob Burckhardt said of the medieval schoolmen that "a glow of the supernatural overshadowed them," and the same may be said of the Reformers. It gave them an inward stability and wholeness which characterized their total outlook.

The development of modern scholarship demonstrates

tragically what happens when these ties are severed. If cultural life, particularly scientific inquiry, emancipates itself from its spiritual moorings nothing can prevent its degradation into mere techniques for practical purposes. Secularism is the death blow to every creative activity, so that not even the most exact sciences, physics and chemistry, can preserve their creativeness once they become isolated from a total philosophy of existence. Thereafter they are mere servants to satisfy the ever-changing demands of the moment.

It is, moreover, impossible to divide knowledge into various independent, self-sufficient departments; everything here is closely interrelated. If the scholar in only one field is prevented from reaching out for the truth (and truth is always in some way divine truth), his creative ability will in time decline.

There are other reasons why we must clearly distinguish between the modern axiom of the freedom of science—the empirical detachment of scientific investigation—and the freedom of the spirit which the Reformation championed.

"Empiricism" always carries a negative connotation. Originally it was contrasted with the dark Middle Ages. Who is the target today? What kind of dogmatic interference hampers the modern scholar? Since "clericalism" no longer dominates the scene (it is no secret that it disappeared several centuries ago), one wonders who the modern enemies of a "free scientific inquiry" really are.

Another factor has much graver implications. This orientation threatens to cut science off from life. It is highly desirable that no one should harass the chemist who proclaims that water is H_2O. But even during the most barren periods of mechanistic thinking, no serious chemist believed that this formula exhausted all the properties of water, let alone explained the quality of the universe.

It is well known that all sciences rely on hypotheses. For the last two generations physicists have carried on their work on the assumption that their concept of the "physical universe" was accurate, but this concept is now undergoing apparently revolutionary changes.

In similar fashion, the jurist, the physician, the economist have practiced their professions on the basis of a total world view which had appeared valid in their particular branches of knowledge. It is absurd to demand that every scholar should or could begin his own work with an investigation of the basic premises of his special science. It is especially naive to assume that scientific theology is only possible if the theologian attempts to place himself outside of the Christian faith, as though he did not share that faith or had not even heard about it.

It is also true that no one treated the vaunted "empirical freedom" as lightly as its first advocates. They were as a rule particularly biased. Were there not numerous representatives of the natural sciences who insisted unequivocally that the objects of faith were unreal, because they could not be established by their methods or integrated into their specialized fields of knowledge? The "dogmatic prejudices" of the scholastics were never more vehement than the intellectual intolerance of a generation which consistently discarded whatever did not conform to the standards of one "infallible" science.

This "progress" itself has already become history, a past phase over which the grass has grown, and a new science of the universe is emerging, characterized by a fundamentally changed outlook, which is still in the process of formulation. That makes it all the more important to revise distorted views still widely held about the Reformation attitude towards science.

What is the real contribution that Protestantism has made to contemporary civilization?

The Reformation unquestionably secured freedom for science and the activities of the intellect. While a critical attitude had gained much ground before the Reformation, and the humanists had consistently fostered this spirit, it was the Reformation which inspired the amazing growth of science and research in subsequent centuries. This development owed its impetus to the "personal thinking" of the Reformation. An individual who knows that he stands in solitary responsibility before God learns to become independent of human authorities. The conviction of having roots in God and the corresponding sense of freedom from human dictation have inspired almost all great spiritual achievements which followed in the wake of the Reformation.

The first science to benefit by this new attitude was the one in which the Reformers were most immediately interested —theology. The change here extended even to methods. Luther devoted his lectures no longer to the traditional exegesis of scholastic writers, but presented his students with the results of his own researches and discussions with other theologians. He took literally the humanist motto, "back to the sources." He opened the way for a critical examination of the biblical texts, the history of the church, the dogma itself. Even Catholic theologians who still regret that Luther emancipated theology from ecclesiastical tradition must admit that the truly momentous results of modern theological scholarship would have been impossible otherwise.

The nineteenth century presented theology with a new problem. At a time when the historical approach prevailed, it became customary to examine the content of Christianity by methods which secular historians had developed in another field and for other purposes—historical criticism. To the degree that this fundamentally different procedure was employed for theological purposes, the risk of losing the substance of Christianity was increased. But later mistakes cannot detract from the merits of a good beginning.

No other scholarly pursuit was as thoroughly vitalized by the Reformation as the writing of history. It became preeminently the science of Protestantism. The first attempt to write a universal history of mankind from the Protestant point of view was made in the sixteenth century. The author of the colossal work was Flacius Illyricus, the courageous and brilliant representative of Lutheranism in Magdeburg. No one else tried his hand at such an ambitious task for the next two centuries, until the philosopher Leibnitz directed his efforts towards the writing of another "History of the World."

Melanchthon, Sleidan[8] and the Swiss government official, Gilg Tschudi (1505-72),[9] are among the founders of modern historiography, and the study of history has always been cultivated by Protestant scholarship. A direct line leads from Leibnitz to Herder[10]. They are unthinkable, except in a Protestant environment.

---

[8] Johannes Philippi Sleidanus (1507-1556) lawyer, who represented the legal interests of the Protestants at Schmalkalden, wrote a history of the Reformation based largely upon excerpts from official documents. (Tr.)

[9] Dr. Lilje differs from Eduard Fueter, author of the monumental *History of Modern Historiography,* Muenchen 1925. Professor Fueter describes Tschudi as a lifelong opponent of Protestantism and as a tendentious, pro-Catholic writer, whose histories are brilliant in style but careless and partisan in the use of sources. (Tr.)

[10] Johann Gottfried Herder (1744-1803) versatile theologian and churchman, contemporary of Goethe and Schiller at Weimar. Wrote *Ideas Concerning a Philosophy of the History of Mankind.* He sees the development of humanity as a process of education guided by a higher power. Great emphasis is placed upon the indigenous character of national cultures. (Tr.)

More immediate and permanent was the effect of Protestantism upon the educational institutions of Germany. Many ingenious suggestions came originally from Luther, but the real credit belongs to Melanchthon. The schools which were organized by Protestant public authorities in the sixteenth century mark the beginning of a new era in education and become a distinct field for Protestant activity. In making such a claim, we do not ignore the progressive and therefore highly effective educational system which was afterward developed under Jesuit auspices.

Yet pedagogy became to such a degree a preoccupation of Lutheranism that it eventually tended to become a temptation. The desire to guard the purity of doctrine led to an overestimation of reasoning and theorizing. Whenever the vital contact of education with the life of the church and congregation was severed, the danger which always lurks in Protestantism became an evil. It turned to intellectualization. But once more we must emphasize that the faults of a later generation cannot discredit the genuine achievements of an earlier period. Philosophy and jurisprudence, even the natural sciences—one need only recall Copernicus and Kepler—reaped rich benefits from the opportunities which the Reformation had provided for them.

Was not this newly stirred intellectual life, this springtime of the spirit which suddenly flourished everywhere, broken into too many isolated fragments? Was not the unity of the world view, the marvelous synthesis of medieval thought, lost in a multitude of colorful details? Could Lutheranism replace the impressive spiritual monism of medieval Catholicism? For the moment we overlook the fact that this unity no longer existed in the late Middle Ages, because the Catholic view of the universe was questioned on so many scores that its integrity was seriously threatened.

The question whether Luther could provide this kind of unity can be answered with an unqualified, Yes. Such unity did actually exist. During Luther's lifetime the University of Wittenberg attracted students from every country. Luther was indeed more than merely the *praeceptor Germaniae.* The gradual decline of this university during a time when teachers of the caliber of Abraham Calov (1650) who shared the Reformer's fighting spirit but little else, occupied the chair of theology, is a sad chapter in the history of developing Lutheranism.

However, Wittenberg's failure brought another Saxon university into prominence. A Lutheran atmosphere prevailed at Jena and its influence was felt in all departments of the humanities, particularly in philosophy. It was outwardly symbolized by the fact that all professors signed the *Formula of Concord.* No one felt that this regulation involved intellectual coercion or the curtailment of academic freedom. They no more considered religion incompatible with philosophy than did Descartes, the founder of modern philosophy, whose scientific determinism did not prevent him from writing an essay in defense of the Eucharist. In fact nowhere else was the genius of Lutheranism as ably and forcefully represented as by the members of the faculty of philosophy at Jena.

Just as Jena had taken over the declining prestige of Wittenberg, philosophy now moved into the gap which had been left by traditional Lutheran theology. The recognized leader of this very influential school of philosophy was Christian Frederick Wolff (1679-1754). Posterity has frequently misjudged him. Because his pupils transformed his philosophy into the religion of the Enlightenment, Wolff has usually been portrayed as the father of German deism. Wolff did not consider himself a rationalist. He wanted to be a loyal

Lutheran, who endeavored to incorporate the content of the Lutheran confessions into a system of metaphysics. He was the first philosopher to use the German language in his writings, and thereby created not only a German philosophical terminology but a philosophical temperament. Anyone who has ever been conscious of the subtle influence of language upon thought will realize what Wolff's substitution of German for Latin meant. It was more than an exchange of one set of technical terms for another. In his straightforward, crystal-clear style, which is never brilliant but always precise, he laid the foundation for the future great systems of German idealism. There is no gainsaying that they were Lutheran foundations.

The influence of Wolff's philosophy extended far. In lecture halls and pulpits his students used his language and proclaimed his thoughts. Catholic philosophy of the time was completely overshadowed by the dominant influence of Wolff.

The greatest intellectual genius of the age, towering above all other leaders of thought, was Gottfried Wilhelm Leibnitz.[11] Ecumenical in his thought, conciliatory towards the old church, he was the most brilliant and versatile representative of the Lutheran spirit. He combined in his person all the forces and tendencies which raised the Lutheran civilization of the seventeenth century to a high level of intellectual achievement. A naturalist and theologian, historian and philosopher, linguist and mathematician, his contemporaries called him a one-man academy of sciences. This universality

---

[11] Gottfried Wilhelm Leibnitz (1646-1716), born in Leipsic, son of a university professor, studied law, entered upon a diplomatic career, best known as the author of the theory of monads and the preestablished harmony, which attempted to solve the body-mind relationship. Professor Troeltsch described it as "a system which emphasizes the supremacy of the spirit over nature." (Tr.)

of interests which made Leibnitz the last great European is inseparable from his spirituality. He was as vitally concerned with the great issues that confronted the Christian church as he was about mineralogy, genealogy, theology, philosophy, jurisprudence, and science. To the Prussian Academy of Sciences and Letters he assigned the task of "propagating the gospel through science." He was in constant communication with the Catholic hierarchy, and corresponded regularly with Jacob Spener, the founder of pietism. His deepest feelings are best revealed in a tender Good Friday hymn which is unfortunately almost unknown. He stands for us as a symbol of hope and encouragement. The secularization of the sciences has blighted civilization. The growing isolation of each science from all others, the refinement of techniques which makes the various specialties almost unintelligible to all but their initiates, has dissolved the unity of the Western world. Men are anxiously longing to be free of this departmentalization of life. The sciences are taking heart once more and reach out for a comprehensive view of the universe. Leibnitz, as the last great universal spirit, reminds us of the loss that civilization suffered when it sabotaged the spiritual foundations of life.

The loss is most noticeable in the world of the arts. Burckhardt, who took a generally unfavorable view of the Reformation, is also very critical when he considers its influence upon the arts. He insists that the Reformation retarded their development for centuries. It could not do much harm to German literature because there was little to harm. But the fine arts suffered irreparable damage. Burckhardt is very partial in his judgment. It is, of course, a fact that painting and sculpture were adversely affected by the Reformation. The incentive to erect sacred statues or employ artists for painting scenes from the lives of the saints declined, together with other forms of "pious works." But the art of the Cranachs, father and son, Hans Baldung (Grien), and particularly Dürer refutes Burckhardt's argument. Truly creative ability cannot be crushed by circumstances; the art of portrait painting was born. More than a century elapsed before the spirit of the Reformation found expression in the masterly art of Rembrandt. It is characteristic of Burckhardt that he displays the same bias here. The great historian of art spoke rather slightingly of Rembrandt when he compared him with the artist for whom he had a lifelong admiration, Peter Paul Rubens (1577-1640). This temporary recession is part of the price mankind must always pay for its great spiritual revolutions because there are casualties and other losses even in the wars of the mind.

Music is the form of art which has always been the most adequate medium for the artistic expression of the Protestant genius. The church of the Reformation is a singing church. The Huguenots sang their psalm tunes, the Lutherans their chorales. The chorale, a unique blending of doctrine, adoration, praise, spirited word, and inspiring melody, is as old as the Reformation itself. The hymnal is one of the earliest and most original creations of Lutheranism. The hymns became the forerunners of the truly great, essentially Lutheran musical forms of art—the cantata, the oratorio, the passions. Bach's art is built upon the chorale. When his tremendous musical power was combined with Paul Gerhardt's tender lyrics, the result was an artistic achievement of such perfection that men shall never see its equal. Bach's own art, and the inspiration that has come through him to other composers down through the years, is still alive and strong today, a moving and continually effective expression of Lutheran piety through music.

We must turn to the effect of Protestantism upon the

social order. Max Weber[12] traced the modern capitalistic system to the direct influence of Calvinism. Luther must be definitely credited with the prevention of a breakdown of the social order in the sixteenth century. "Pious works" were the means by which the medieval church coped with the problems of social disorganization. To give to the needy and the beggars assured the giver of great religious merit. Alms were distributed among the poor and the orphans. A special order, the monks and nuns, kept this obligation before the eyes of the public and helped thereby materially to soften the harshness which prevailed in the medieval attitude toward men and social conditions. It is this combination of chivalry with Christianity which finally led to the ideal of the "gentleman." At the moment when "pious works" became religiously meaningless or even harmful, one of the supporting pillars in the social structure collapsed overnight. A device which had regulated the relationship between rich and poor, sick and well, gentry and commoner for centuries, now ceased to function. One is amazed at the rapidity and extent of this breakdown. In large measure it can be attributed to the familiar human tendency to seize upon any excuse that will make plain selfishness respectable. But the reasons go deeper; the breakdown reveals how greatly the traditional social order and the old piety had already deteriorated.

Luther was not content merely to castigate this rising wave of selfishness and remind people that charity was still an essential element of the Christian faith. He counteracted by

---

[12] Max Weber (1864-1920), German professor of law and economics, wrote extensively on the sociology of religion. Economic and social conditions are created by mental activities; religious convictions influence the type of society that given cultures develop for themselves. Weber thus analyzed the social life of the ancient Hebrews, the Chinese, and the Indians, as well as Calvinistic and Puritan societies, to show the influence which various religions had upon the types of social order which they evolved. (Tr.)

offering an ingenious new plan of Christian social action. The aim of charity is the independence of the individual; the helpless must be trained to help themselves. This principle, now an axiom in social work, was new and revolutionary when Luther first proposed it in the introduction to the poor box regulations of 1523. This pamphlet, which Luther had prepared at the request of the magistrates of Leisnig, assures this little village in Saxony of the distinction of being the first community in Europe where a new philosophy of social service replaced the tottering medieval order.

Closely allied with this phase is the rise of a new national consciousness. It had slowly developed through the preceding two centuries and caused repeated outbreaks of violence in the fifteenth century. It came forcefully into its own when the European nations found themselves independent of the protecting mother church. Protestantism, particularly Lutheranism, pays its tribute to wholesome national pride by its respect for the most precious instrument of nationality, the language. The vernacular breathes another spirit than the language of a universal institution—the Latin ritual of the Catholic Church. Luther's faith is couched in the common speech, his hymns and prayers are uttered in words familiar to the man in the street. The trend towards the vernacular was not restricted to German-speaking Protestantism. A century after the superb translation of the Bible into German and the publication of a catechism and hymns in the native tongue, there appeared a translation of the Bible into the wonderfully rich and expressive language of Shakespeare.

More remarkable, though less known, are the changes which Protestantism wrought among the Slavs whose lands border on Russia. These changes can only be compared with more recent events on the foreign mission field. The translation of the Bible into the national languages became the means by which these groups achieved a sense of national consciousness. If the Reformation appeared to many in western Europe like the bright dawn of a new day, the glow was even more brilliant in the east.

Only great care in the investigation of the lines that lead from the Reformation to these new forms of communal life will guard against the popular notion that the Reformation "emancipated" the social order, established it as an independent entity, and thereby secularized it. In the field of social welfare it is said to have paved the way for a secular type of philanthropy. Purely humanitarian, these agencies no longer cared what, if anything, a man believed. They offered the very rich a chance to relieve any possible qualms of conscience over the abundance of their riches by contributing to "charity." The recipients of such "charity" were thereby often goaded into bitter hatred of the Reformation.

This misunderstanding of Luther's attitude toward national life has caused even more serious harm. It has been maintained that Lutheranism represents a "Germanic" type of piety, though this assertion ignores completely the third article of the Creed, and denies the universality of the gospel message that salvation has come to all men through Christ. The corresponding misconception, which accompanies it as shadow accompanies light, is the claim that the Reformation will remain incomplete until the Christian message is divorced from the Old Testament and established as a purely Germanic religion.

Such fundamental misunderstandings of the political and social aims of the Reformation are bound to arise if one sees the movement as a sweeping attempt to secularize the whole of life. Luther did, indeed, transfer the care of the needy from the church to the community, as a routine task of organized communal life. To provide the poor with the necessities of life was no longer a particularly meritorious act but an obvious Christian service, which had to be extended to everyone "without any merit or worthiness." The substitution of the German language for the stately, majestic Latin of the Catholic worship was not an attempt to secularize the faith but to bring God close to men.

Not secularization, but the actualization of the Christian life was the deepest concern of the Reformation. Where God becomes real, the practice of the Christian ethos is always felt as a present and concrete obligation. Charity is not a mere adjunct to life, one more ornament in addition to others, but an integral element in the life situation itself. All men owe their existence to God, they are his beneficiaries, and only human shortsightedness differentiates between those who have and those who are in need. Because all the goods of life come to me as divine gifts, I have no right to withhold anything or claim it as a personal possession. This fact is strikingly set forth in the parable of the Good Samaritan. The scribe had raised the question: Who is my neighbor? Christ reversed the question by asking the scribe: "Which thinkest thou was neighbor unto him who fell among the thieves?" How would you have judged if you had been the victim? The fact that we are, without exception, recipients of God's gifts, constitutes all of us as members of a universal community. This solidarity must determine our actions and motivate our "charities." If we begin with this premise, charity is no longer benevolent condescension but the affirmation of our human fellowship. The nature and extent of the ethical obligation is no longer a subject for philosophical speculation. The obligation presents itself in ever-present, real-life situations from which I cannot escape. It is no longer a matter of personal choice, whether I wish to add charity to other manifestations of my Christian life, but—to use Christ's own words—I am at all times neighbor to some person and some person is neighbor to me. We never live to ourselves. From the moment of birth we stand in relation of mutual neighborliness to others. Parents have children and children have parents. On a large scale the same situation prevails throughout the community and nation. Life becomes real, once we have recognized this fact. God steadily confronts the individual, and this confrontation occurs through other people and in concrete life situations. My "I" is always in contact with "Another" who represents God's will and command for me. That is meant by the "actualization" of the gospel. It is, in the most literal sense, the only hope we have to reconstruct our crumbling human relationships, of rebuilding community spirit and community responsibility out of the chaos of the "mass destiny" in which we have become involved.

This is not the place to discuss Luther's often misunderstood orientation towards his native Germany. He felt deeply for the land of his birth and often expressed his love for it, but these utterances are quite unsuited for the construction of any theory or theology of nationalism. There is not the slightest indication that he considered the Germans a "chosen" people or had any illusions about a specifically "Germanic" religion. Here, as elsewhere, his one wish was to make God real to men. He, therefore, desired God's call to come to men in the one language they knew from infancy, the language which was as familiar to them as the air they breathed.

When the great humanist Erasmus lay dying in Basle, he whispered his last words in his native Dutch: *Lieve God.* The man who had written and spoken Latin almost all his life, who had made the language of ancient Rome a living means of communication among the intellectuals of Europe, uttered his last simple prayer in his mother tongue. That is it: God speaks to me here and now, in the reality of my everyday surroundings, rather than in some sublime grandeur that bears little relationship to my actual existence. We, likewise, draw near unto God out of the realities of our lives, once we have heard and heeded his call.

That is the "secularism" of the Reformation which has been so often extolled and more often misunderstood. It was not an attempt to "recapture" the world. The "world," which has a rightful place in the Christian scheme of things, could not be lost, and was largely preserved even in the Catholic order, though some modern extremists will find it difficult to realize that fact. It was the supreme aim of the Reformation to make God real, here and now, so that people would be compelled to take him seriously. One of the crudest, most common errors is the notion that Protestantism wished to liberate men from the church, so that he is the best Protestant who never goes to church. The opposite is true: a good Protestant worships God by his total Christian life, Sundays and weekdays, in church and out of church. Worldly piety—yes; if it is genuine piety it cannot be anything else. But this piety is not the end of the era of the church but its extension, until it claims all men, and the whole of life and existence becomes worship.

The Problem of
Tomorrow

Our survey is completed, but one crucial question remains;
it casts doubt and uncertainty over everything that has been
said so far. It becomes an even more disturbing question if
we admit that the past four centuries, as we have reviewed
them, constitute an organic unit, a closely interrelated epoch
in human history. We ask ourselves whether all these events
are not irrevocably swallowed up in history, a past which has
slipped through our hands and can never be brought back
to life. Some readers will undoubtedly be interested in historical information and might appreciate the correction of
certain false impressions about the Reformation, but in the
long run it makes little difference whether this or some other
interpretation of the facts is more accurate. For all this is
history; it is past, a closed chapter in the long pilgrimage of
the human mind. Every indication points to the probability
that the question of tomorrow will not be "Catholicism or
Protestantism?" but "Can the Christian heritage be preserved?" For many this has even ceased to be a question. They
are convinced that the age of Christianity itself is on the
wane. Unless a study of the Reformation is to serve purely
academic interests, we must face this question resolutely, without minimizing its implications. Every objective appraisal of
the situation leads to the conclusion that the Christian era

is nearing its end or has already passed. The "Christian era" was the age of Constantine. Constantine's choice put the Christian church into a position where it could create and mold the "Western" world view. A fully occidental civilization did not arise until the European nations, particularly the migrating Germanic tribes, made their first extended contacts with the Christian church. The emergence of a "Christian era" presented the church with entirely new problems. A persecuted, insignificant minority had suddenly become the majority. If it had formerly been the exception to belong to the Christian church, membership now became the rule. To be a Christian no longer called for a personal decision but had become routine. The church itself was transformed from a missionary into a teaching church. Christianity's loss was Europe's gain. Christianity paid a heavy price for its new position as schoolmaster of Europe, probably the most gigantic educational undertaking in all history. The fervor of the personal conversion became weakened, the hope for the *parousia* grew dim. The Christian community was no longer a small flock in the world, but the Christian world itself, *orbis christianus.*

In order to make these rich contributions to European life, the church impoverished itself. It helped Europe achieve spiritual consolidation and such inner strength and resourcefulness, in the process, as has never been the good fortune of any other continent. Culture, customs, artistic tastes became unified throughout Europe. A Romanesque chapel in an Italian town looked exactly like its counterpart in Aix-la-Chapelle or Fulda. With the exception of slight, nationally determined variations, the great Gothic cathedrals show the same design, whether they stand in Exeter, Cologne, Prague, or Paris. This unification of civilization was based upon a common faith. Novalis was right when he spoke of "Christianity or Europe."

Every member of the European civilization was automatically a Christian. The only exception were the Jews and the Moors of Spain, and people felt that they were foreign elements. For the past two centuries this solid foundation has been attacked by corrosion; slowly, almost imperceptibly in the beginning, but gathering momentum, until in the nineteenth century individuals and small groups openly rejected the Christian social order. It has remained for powerful new movements in the twentieth century to agitate the total rejection of Christianity and substitute their own ideologies as spiritual dynamics for Western civilization. It is probably a fact that the quiet secularization during the last century has done greater harm than the open revolt of the present. The outcome, however, can no longer be in doubt. The era when Europe was a Christian continent lies behind us.

The new situation is not necessarily fatal to Christianity. The many opportunities to influence public life were as many opportunities to compromise the gospel, and the church has too often succumbed to the temptation. History now forces the church back into the conditions which prevailed at her beginnings. The church of tomorrow will be more like the early church than has been the case for many centuries. It will be a missionary church rather than a civilizing factor. As "the little flock" she will draw inspiration and strength from her Lord rather than from her harmonious adjustment to the cultural pattern. The change is already apparent. Church membership will become more a matter of personal choice than social custom. Ranke had already observed the role of discrimination over tradition, since the two churches existed in Europe side by side. That applies in an even more fundamental sense today, when it is no longer a question as to which church one wishes to belong, but whether one wants church at all. The church itself stands to gain when its membership is no longer largely made up of "conventional Christians" but loyal disciples and witnesses. It will be the kind of church for which so ardent and conscientious a spirit as Kierkegaard longed all his life.

The perhaps permanent loss of official standing in European life need not be a loss for Christianity. The Christian who is familiar with his New Testament knows that the church at the end of its earthly career will again resemble the apostlic church, and that the promises of the Lord were given to "the little flock."

The truly fateful question is rather addressed to Western civilization. Will it cut itself loose from its own past, the foundations on which it has rested? We must admit that the reconstruction of European civilization on a non-Christian basis is theoretically possible. Until now, however, all attempts in that direction have been unsuccessful. Can Europe really preserve or recapture its spiritual unity under a new aegis? It seems very unlikely, though all (or perhaps because all) efforts at reconstruction call for the unconditional surrender of the individual to a totalitarian order. Can life be worth living under such a system? At the moment one must reserve the answer. Meanwhile the one specter which the nineteenth century seemed to have banned forever recurs in all its viciousness: religious wars under the disguise of political decisions. On blood-drenched battlefields Europe seeks to decide what its future shall be. The Christian cannot retreat to a neutral position. He must give his answer to the question, "Can one really hope or wish that the new Europe should return to the spiritual foundations of the Reformation?"

The problem is not the "revival" of Christianity. Faith in Christ has flourished in the Roman Empire, under the Germanic rulers, during the Middle Ages, the modern era, and there will always be men and women who will find their way to Christ, even in the iron age of the dictators.

It becomes our task to make the faith of the Reformation so real to our contemporaries that they recognize its timelessness and its relevancy to our present predicament. The faith of the Reformation touches directly upon the gravest needs of our own day. We cannot, of course, return to the Reformation, as though one could erase the passing of the centuries. We cannot even return to any other "Protestant orientation" (for instance Kierkegaard), even though it be chronologically closer to our own age. We must experience the faith in our particular situation, as the Reformers experienced it in theirs. In one respect that situation was strangely like our own. If we refer to it as Luther's personal experience, we do so because he felt it more keenly and deeply than any of his contemporaries. His plight, like ours, is a profound sense of the uncertainty of human existence. We are not secure in this world, but in constant peril. At the very moment in which it dawned upon Luther that the practices of the church offered no protection against the horrors of hell and the accusations of his own conscience, the old world and the old church lay shattered at his feet. The security which the church offered was only an apparent security. The protecting walls which she had built around him crumbled into dust, and he stood defenseless before the wrath of God. It was God himself who had called him for judgment and placed his life in jeopardy.

It was then that a wonderful new insight came to Luther: God himself threatened his existence, but when Luther appeared before this God, who could cause his extinction, he realized that God always preserved him. The sinner becomes justified, God permits man to live before him, though man has forfeited his existence. Man no longer tries to evade the divine judgment by every kind of artifice but accepts judgment, knowing full well that he can only survive as sinner. *Simul iustus et peccator.* Christ becomes our assurance of divine forgiveness.

Our present outlook differs fundamentally from the prevailing optimistic world view of the last one hundred and fifty years. We have traumatically experienced the threat that hangs over human existence. We know that, whatever the future may hold, none of the accustomed safeguards and protections will go along with us. The fences and walls that used to shelter us have all broken down. We cannot look for help to academic philosophies or popular treatises on "peace of mind." Not even "religion" can assure safety against the elemental threats of life. The Reformers show us that God himself exposes man to this threat. We are in the presence of God, not of fate. It is therefore meaningless to confront "fate," as though we had the power to meet the challenge.

Job's quest for God's providence and Luther's quest for God's grace merge into the great quest of our own age. Such warnings and earnest admonitions as the great critics of our civilization have voiced for the last one hundred years are no longer sufficient. Job and Luther discovered how futile it is to interrogate God. God himself forces us into the reversed position where we stop asking questions in order to hear his answer. All human roads seek to avoid these deep valleys. It was Luther's experience that God purposely leads us through them in order to make us receptive to his Word.

That has always been so, and, if we are more conscious of it than the men and women of the last few generations, we are also more ready for the divine benediction that can transform and bless all our agonies.

Amidst the distress and unspeakable anguish of our age,

the presence of Christ and of God's forgiving, restoring grace will become the more manifest.

Europe faces once more the hour of decision. If its soul and faith have been forever lost, it will not recover.

Type used in this book
Body, 11 on 12 Garamond
Display, Garamond bold